SWIRLING

Imagine being at your favorite ice cream shop and sampling each irresistible flavor—not just chocolate, vanilla, or strawberry, but Mexican fried ice cream, Japanese green tea, a French glacé, or an Italian gelato. Now imagine your dating life being that same kind of scrumptious smorgasbord with someone of a different race, religion, or culture. Sound delicious? Then *Swirling: How to Date, Mate, and Relate Mixing Race, Culture, and Creed* is your must-read book!

Swirling is the straight-from-the-source guidebook that informs women about the sometimes awkward, tricky, or even frightening terrain of dating someone outside your race, culture, or faith. Filled with amusing real-life stories from stalwart *swirlers*—some inspiring, some horrifying, others wonderfully hilarious—*Swirling* also blends first-hand testimonials from the authors with an assortment of tips, lists, and devices that will open your eyes to the splendor of meeting, dating . . . and even walking down the aisle with the man of your dreams.

Early Praise for **SWIRLING**

"A welcome, heartfelt primer on what African American women can and should do to better prepare themselves for the challenges, frustrations, as well as the possibilities and hopes in the turbulent world of relationships. It's a book whose time has more than come."

—EARL OFARI HUTCHINSON
nationally syndicated columnist, author, and social commentator

"Janice Rhoshalle Littlejohn and Christelyn D. Karazin bring a refreshing perspective to this hotly debated and newsworthy topic—they also have the journalistic mettle and personal experience and humor to pull off a book that is both entertaining and informational.... A must-read."

—BRIAN LOWRY
Variety *chief television critic*

"This surprising and oh-so-timely book should be considered essential reading for any woman who feels rudderless when it comes to finding a soul mate . . . smartly researched and eye-opening."

—JOHN GRIFFITHS
Us Weekly *television critic*

"After nearly 20 years in an interracial marriage, the one thing I've learned is that black folks often have more hang-ups about these kinds of relationships than anyone else. And if anyone can help us sort through the nonsense, problems, and preconceptions, it is Janice Rhoshalle Littlejohn—one of the smartest, most empathetic writers I know. I only hope she starts on a book for black men next!"

—ERIC DEGGANS

TV/Media Critic, Tampa Bay Times

"Wisely written . . . smart, conversational and honest."

—MEKEISHA MADDEN TOBY

The Detroit News

"What an important and timely topic! Karazin and Littlejohn's warm conversational style sets the perfect tone for women in interracial and intercultural relationships who are seeking practical advice and support."

—LINDA R. YOUNG, PhD

psychologist and blogger for Psychology Today

"A breath of fresh air."

—CHERILYN "CW" SMITH

popular blogger and author of Black Women Deserve Better

"Couldn't come at a better time."

—LECIA J. BROOKS

Director, Civil Rights Memorial Center, Southern Poverty Law Center

SWIRLING

How to Date, Mate,
and Relate Mixing Race,
Culture, and Creed

Christelyn D. Karazin
and
Janice Rhoshalle Littlejohn

ATRIA PAPERBACK
New York · London · Toronto · Sydney · New Delhi

ATRIA PAPERBACK

A Division of Simon & Schuster, Inc.
1230 Avenue of the Americas
New York, NY 10020

First Atria Paperback edition May 2012

ATRIA PAPERBACK and colophon are trademarks of Simon & Schuster, Inc.

For information about special discounts for bulk purchases,
please contact Simon & Schuster Special Sales at 1-866-506-1949 or
business@simonandschuster.com.

The Simon & Schuster Speakers Bureau can bring authors to your live event. For
more information or to book an event, contact the Simon & Schuster Speakers
Bureau at 1-866-248-3049 or visit our website at www.simonspeakers.com.

Designed by Dana Sloan

Manufactured in the United States of America

10 9 8 7 6 5 4 3 2 1

Library of Congress Cataloging-in-Publication Data is available upon request.

ISBN 978-1-4516-2585-1
ISBN 978-1-4516-2586-8 (ebook)

For my dedicated husband, Michael, who fanned that little matchlight of an idea and made me do it till it was done.

To Kayla, Chloe, Zachary, and Emma:
Mommy loves you so very, very much.

For Mom, who is the best teacher of pot stirring I've ever seen.

For Dad, who always, always believed in me when the rest of the world thought I was hopeless.
Until heaven, I will miss you.

—CHRISTELYN D. KARAZIN

For my parents:
Thank you for believing in me even when understanding me proved difficult. I love you both.

For my nieces, nephews, and godchildren:
Live bravely,
Love openly,
Choose wisely.

—JANICE RHOSHALLE LITTLEJOHN

CONTENTS

AUTHORS' NOTE   xiii

INTRODUCTION

Christelyn's Story: Jumping the Broom with a White Boy   1

PART I: BLACK WOMEN DESERVE A GOOD LOVE, TOO

CHAPTER ONE

Christelyn | Deprogram: Unthink Everything You've Ever Assumed About Swirling   11

CHAPTER TWO

Janice | Who's Swirling?   25

CHAPTER THREE

Janice | Best U.S. Cities That Swirl   41

CHAPTER FOUR

Christelyn | Feel Like You Need Permission to Swirl? Girl, You Got It.   51

CHAPTER FIVE

Christelyn | Is It Time to Edit the List?   63

CHAPTER SIX

Christelyn | How to Go from Mr. Rainbeau to Mr. Right   75

PART II: PUT YOURSELF OUT THERE

CHAPTER SEVEN

Janice | Why It's Worth It   97

CHAPTER EIGHT

Janice | You've Decided. Now Get Busy: 52 Ways
to Find a Date   109

CHAPTER NINE

Janice | The Rules of Flirtation: Knowing When
He's Interested   129

CHAPTER TEN

Janice | The First Date: Finding Neutral Ground   149

CHAPTER ELEVEN

Janice | Moving Forward . . . Or Moving On   159

CHAPTER TWELVE

Janice | Let's Talk About Sex . . . and Stereotypes   165

PART III: WHEN IT GETS REALLY SERIOUS

CHAPTER THIRTEEN

Christelyn | Love Is Blind . . . But Not Those People
Staring at You!   185

CHAPTER FOURTEEN

Christelyn | Dealing with Conflicting Loyalties   197

CHAPTER FIFTEEN

Christelyn | Handling the *Guess Who's Coming
to Dinner* Moment   215

CONTENTS

CHAPTER SIXTEEN

Christelyn | Time to Decide: Is It All Worth It?   227

AFTERWORD

Janice's Story: And She Lived Happily Ever After . . .   231

ACKNOWLEDGMENTS   247

RESOURCES   253

AUTHORS' NOTE

Some of the best stories start with an unexpected phone call that changes everything. In this case, the call came from Christelyn. On the other end of the line, she was breathless and talking faster than her normal rapid-fire gabbing. She was excited, ecstatic really. Having just returned from New York days before, where she had attended a conference of the American Society of Journalists and Authors, she had been pitching a story to literary agents about how she came to marry her husband, a story that she had pitched to *Elle* earlier that year, a personal essay she thought the editors might be receptive to. And while there was one that did, the piece never made it through the editorial labyrinth at the haughty New York glossy. So she began suggesting it as a book on how to go about dating interracially. (I'll say this for Chris: She is nothing if not doggedly persistent.) Her resolve was rewarded: three agents wanted to see the book proposal—which she had not yet written. "I want you to write it with me," she said.

"Why me?" I asked. In my mind, this story was hers, not mine.

"You have discipline and stamina. I need you to be my security blanket to make sure that I get it done," she said, after spreading the honey-coated compliments about my skills as a writer. "And with your contacts in the publishing industry, and my writing style—which you could complement well—I really think we could do something great.

"Plus, I can't write a book by myself—not the *whole* damn thing!"

For many reasons, I wanted to say no—not the least of which that I had just written a two-hundred-and-fifteen-page novel not less than two years prior, my thesis project in graduate school (it has not yet been published); researching and writing it almost buried me, even though I had decided to spin off the idea into a documentary film, for which I had just finished writing and editing a sixteen-page treatment.

That, and I wanted my first book to have my name on it alone. I felt that after twenty years as a writer, I had earned that vanity point.

And yet, as a single African American woman, now divorced for more than a dozen years, I felt I had something to say on the subject of interracial and crosscultural romances. Just weeks before Chris's call, I had read a study about how black women were the least likely of any ethnic group to marry and the myriad reasons why, including the reluctance to dating out. But for me, the timing was right on a personal level. I was looking to jump into the dating pool again a little more seriously, having ended a relationship that, quite honestly, should have never begun in the first place and went on much too long, creating too much residual pain; requiring a lot of therapy-induced introspection and evenings spent with Barbra Streisand's "Stayed Too Long

at the Fair." Sometimes smart women do dumb things in relationships; and as black women, I have found, we are oftentimes
a little clueless when it comes to seeking relationships outside
of our race or ethnic group. This I realize is a generalized statement. But it's also true. As a journalist, I felt it my job to understand the reasons why and to give insight on how to get past it.

So I agreed to coauthor the book with Christelyn.

It surprised her that I said yes so quickly. "I thought I'd have
to negotiate, I thought I'd have to cajole," she told me later, as we
raked through the edits of this book on my living room floor on
a postcard-perfect mid-October afternoon in Los Angeles. "I really thought I'd have to beg and plead for a while because I knew
this was going to be a big undertaking, like godmother-to-my-
children big."

And she's never asked me to do *that*.

It had been sixteen years since we met at Loyola Marymount
University, when I was paired with her as an alumni mentor, she
an eager, wide-eyed sophomore with dreams of becoming a reporter like me; here we are now, writing colleagues with a like-
minded mission: to dare black women to think differently.

That said, this isn't a book that is trying to convince you why
you should date outside your race and culture; there are enough
books, studies, news reports and specials, documentaries, and
"experts" on the subject to tell you that. What we want to do is
help you do it.

Dating out can be wonderfully sublime. But for the novice,
it can be daunting and intimidating. And we've both been there,
with differing degrees on the outcome. In us, you get the per-

spectives of a woman who found marital bliss with someone of another race, and another happy to date a rainbow of men without the down-the-aisle end game. Playing to both our strengths and interests, my chapters tackle such topics as where to find a mate, flirting, dating, and sex, because Christelyn, despite having had four children, is girlishly coy on the topic of coitus. For her part, she wanted to focus on the weighty issues that need to be addressed once the relationship gets into a deeper level when friends and family, and the people staring at you and your rainbeau in the supermarket, begin to play a factor in the relationship.

At the top of each chapter, we have identified those authored by Christelyn, and those I have written. And it is a book you can read out of sequence or in; all are self-contained works giving you the information you want when you need it. Writing *Swirling* has been nothing short of a positively transformative experience for Chris and me; my dating life alone has never been so wildly robust. And in your reading of *Swirling,* we hope, brings a deliciously fruitful and satisfying change in your dating experience.

—*Janice Rhoshalle Littlejohn, with Christelyn D. Karazin*

SWIRLING

Christelyn's Story

Jumping the Broom
with a White Boy

Marriage is for white people.

It's hard to say what I felt exactly when I read that *Washington Post* editorial a few years ago—offended, outed, but mostly just sad. Finally, writer Joy Jones had exposed the furtive secret, the dirty laundry. Despite the fact that my own parents had been married for forty-five years, I learned early that marriage for whites and blacks was distinctly different. In my pubescent, wide-eyed youth, I remember the image I had was of hands clasped against one cheek, me sighing dreams of love, marriage, mutual understanding and cooperation. I would relate them to some friend or relative only for them to scoff, "That's some fairy-tale-white-people-shit."

If black women—regardless of class and education—were really honest, most would tell you that their ideal mate is a black

1

man. It's only natural to want to be with someone who looks like you. The problem is, the chances are slim—African Americans have the lowest marriage rate of all races, and black women are at the back of the line. I once knew a single black woman with a thriving career as a civil engineer and cofranchiser of a Subway sandwich shop, who told me, "I'm still holding out for my black man." In her church, work, or circle of friends, she could not find one single, solitary black man who could fit the bill. "I don't care if he's a FedEx carrier, I just want a good one," she had said.

We lost touch, so I never found out if the deliveryman ever came knocking with that ring in hand. But if I were a gambler, I'd say she must have faced some tough odds on finding her black man, given a statistic such as 42 percent of black women will never marry, compared to 21 percent of white women.

So, if marriage is for white people, what option does an educated, fertile, marriage-minded black female have? Know this: Prince Charming comes in all colors. It's time to expand your horizons and simply find a *good* man.

I realize that some black women, steadfast in their quest to find the ultimate brother, may bristle when they read this. If they want motherhood, some would rather concede to "babymama" status if they can't get their partner to commit for life, for reasons here too presumptuous of me to assume. I can only speak for myself. My twelve-year-old daughter's father, who is black, outright refused to marry me when I became pregnant in college, despite dangling the marriage carrot in front of my nose for a year prior. His parents never married. His own father has three illegitimate children (that we know of at least). As my belly swelled, I remember being so ashamed that I bought a cubic zirconia to wear on my ring finger when we were out together in public. It didn't bother him a bit. To him, marriage was nonessential.

And still others, like my engineer friend, would rather forfeit marriage and motherhood than ever consider marrying outside their race. It's a betrayal of the Afrocentric us-against-the-world groupthink, and a heartbreaking remnant of slavery. It's the pebble in all our shoes. Marriage for slaves was not legally or spiritually binding by the ruling class. Defiant lovers still found ways to express their eternal devotion by jumping the broom, which symbolized the leap into a new life, and living together. Such "frivolity" did not stop the slave owners and foreman from raping the women, while husbands and sons watched, helpless and impotent. Some of us still have not forgiven.

My husband and I jumped the broom the day we married. My mother insisted on it, perhaps as a not so subtle reminder to me from where I've come. So with clenched teeth and sweaty palms I took the leap with my white husband, and into a world that was neither black nor white, but brushed with of wisps of gray. An interracial marriage is truly risky. You join the ranks of odd couples who abdicate their anonymity and risk ridicule. Tall and short, skinny and portly, black and white. Someone stares a millisecond longer than what is comfortable, and then you wonder. A salesman snubs you and then you speculate. You weren't invited to a party and you can't help but think, Is it because my husband is white?

Is it because I'm black?

I have been called a nigger three times in my life. The first time was in elementary school: a blond boy with dirty clothes and flies perpetually circling his face spat the word at me while I sat on a swing. Then it happened again in high school—some cowardly adolescent thought it was funny to yell out the slur while I was walking alone from school. The last time came just before my wedding.

I was walking alongside a coworker passing out notices to homeowners about freeway work to be done in Costa Mesa, California. We made the best of it, laughing about the ridiculous job, how the execs liked to hand off the grunt work to the juniors. We took in the sunshine. We talked about our significant others. He knew my intended was white, and asked me about it.

"What's it like?" he asked, innocently. "Do you ever worry about what people say?"

"Not at all," I said, full of cosmopolitan bravado. "This is California, not Mississippi."

Almost immediately after, a white pickup blazed passed us, a little too close to the curb. A man hung his elbow out of the window. Then it had happened a third time.

"Nigger!" The cowards hit the gas and zoomed away.

My coworker, who was white, seemed incredulous, almost embarrassed, and a little scared. Then, unsure of what to do, he chuckled nervously, "You're not offended by those jerks, are you? Ha! What jerks!" Then, he looked at me and saw my face, brown and burning, tears swelling against the bridge of my nose. "God, Chris. I'm sorry."

I remember thinking at the time about how absurd it was. Why apologize for what those chumps yelled out? Did he think that I would hold him responsible in some way, like some collective condemnation for all bigots of the world? In a way, he did. In some ways, we all do.

Before that incident I lived in a bubble of self-imposed denial about what it would be like to be married to someone white. I grew up in the 1980s, but I was only one generation removed from drinking out of the "Blacks Only" fountain. That day, something grabbed hold and shook me. I began to overanalyze the incident, rewinding and replaying it. Seeing us laughing and walking together must have looked like intimacy to those men. They must have thought we were on a date.

Later that evening I told my fiancé about it. He kissed my tears. He called the men bastards. Then we went on, one foot in front of the other, down the aisle. Because no matter what, nothing changed the fact that we loved to cook and garden together, and debate the latest news outrage in bed on Sunday mornings. It didn't erase that we completed each other's sentences. He had an uncanny way of reading me and knowing my secrets, and loving me still.

When it was time to take the leap, my palms slick with sweat, part of me was giddy with love and promise; the other, secret part was full of fear and dread. I would begin a life with a man who had never known open prejudice, never been called a name meant to humiliate and dehumanize him. He would have to understand why that word "nigger" had so much power, how it could cause me to crumble into tears. He would have to toughen up to hear a few slurs of his own, now that he was going to be married to me.

At our wedding, I gave one last look at the audience. To my left was his family and friends—mostly white—and to the right was my family. Black sand, white sea foam. As the tide ebbs and flows, each part takes and leaves a little of itself with the other. I looked at my soon-to-be husband, with his wide smile and hopeful green eyes, and I knew in an instant that no matter what the future brought, this was my man. He was the man.

Almost equally ironic as was the drive-by name calling fluke, my husband and I have been lucky thus never to have experienced blatant outrage or bigotry about our biethnic, bicultural relationship. Indeed, the world is changing. At almost twelve, my oldest daughter has never been called a nigger. There are more families that look like us, both in real life and on television. Finally, the ghosts of slavery and all the isms—racism, colorism, classism—that go along with it are being exorcised. Of course we get the furtive looks and stares of bald curiosity or disdain that comes along with being different. And I must admit I still hold my breath when we walk together past a cluster of black men for fear of their stares of disapproval, or worse—words spoken into action, action into deed. Rational or not, I fear the sting of being called a "sellout" just as much as I do the word "nigger."

I sometimes think about that person who once told me that marriage was a fairy tale in which white people cornered the market. They were wrong. Imperfect and glorious, this little black girl got her fairy-tale ending. My marriage works, just not in the confines of tradition or with the ease of anonymity. We continue to transcend together, beyond Jim Crow and the "n" word, beyond the fear of ridicule. Knowing what I do now, I wish I would have told the engineer-slash-sandwich-shop-owner that you just have to snatch love for yourself when it comes knocking, in whatever color or cultural package he's wrapped in. That's the purpose of this book, and my hope is that all who read it will find love, however it arrives.

PART I

Black Women Deserve a Good Love, Too

swirling > present participle, a romantic blending or mixing of two people most often of another race or ethnicity of the other: *The black librarian and Chinese professor have been swirling for years.*

CHAPTER ONE

Christelyn

Deprogram: Unthink Everything You've Ever Assumed About Swirling

I't's no big secret that at least statistically, black women are the loneliest women in America. Lately our solitary station has made for good entertainment, a boon for black-male-comedians-turned-relationship-experts, fodder for TV newsmagazines, radio shows, and seminars—all with chatter and collective wringing of hands that 70 percent of African American women are single according to the latest census date.

Is it a choice?

Have we become so liberated as to be completely self-sufficient, providing for ourselves emotionally, financially, and sexually?

Let's be real, ladies.

There aren't enough church groups, community service activities and girlfriend trips to Vegas to take the place of your one and only. Most of us have a lion's share of familial love, friendship, and Christian sister and brotherhood, but that's not the love I'm talking about. None compares to the strong embrace of the man who adores and accepts you, who cherishes you and is faithful to you even when your breasts start to sag and you discreetly start shopping for Depends. Nothing is more comforting than a life partner who will be that hero for you through thick or thin, kinky or straight.

The lamentable truth is that at least two million of us are in jeopardy of never experiencing that kind of love, especially within our own race. The shortage of black men is real—and black women are fighting like alley cats for the half a handful of eligible and marriageable brothers. As far as I know Denzel Washington cannot (yet) be cloned. So the way I see it, if you're looking for a mate, you've got three choices:

1. Stay single until science figures out how to replicate Mr. Washington's DNA two million times.

2. Scrounge, compete, and put up with outrageous nonsense just so you can at least *say* you have a man—regardless of how he may treat you.

Or

3. Simply change your attitude and open up your dating options outside your race. In short, choose character *above*

color. It's either number 3, or just let your Aunt Harriet set you up with her church friend's son who is forty-five and still lives in his mom's basement, trying to be a rapper.

That means offering up more than just a friendly "hello" to that white accountant who always lights up like Christmas when he sees you at Starbucks. How about actually looking at the geeky but sweet Asian IT guru who's always trying his best to strike up a conversation with you at the copy machine? Perhaps that hot Latino who owns the local flower shop . . . well, you get my drift.

One anonymous poster on askmen.com, said this about black women dating outside their race: "The more races and cultures you're open to, the more [eligible bachelors] there are." Bingo! The black woman's man shortage is solved!

If only.

Despite the documented rise in interracial and intercultural dating and marriage, there is still a lot of resistance within the black community about coupling "outside" the race, and black women get even worse flak for intermixing, which is often viewed as disloyal and self-hating. But answer me this: Is it hating yourself to seek happiness and love with someone who has similar goals, education, and interests? Then so what if he's melanin-challenged or hails from another country? One of the biggest expressions of love for yourself is the understanding that you are worthy of a quality mate.

And tell me, please, where is the loyalty for black women? Black men have married outside their race for decades. Arguably the most famous interracial marriage between a black man and a white woman was Frederick Douglass and his second wife, Helen Pitts, in 1884. Whereas, it was nearly eighty years later when Mildred Loving, a woman of African American and Native American decent, defended her interracial marriage to a white man, Richard Loving, in a celebrated Supreme Court case in 1967.

The good news is that some women are starting to "get it." An informal survey on my blog, BeyondBlackWhite.com, revealed that out of 165 participants, nearly 50 percent of black women between the ages of 18 and 55 said that they are looking for someone who matches their values, education level, and aspirations, whatever color he is.

But still, many black women (including myself at one time) buy into the stereotypes and build up invisible roadblocks that contribute to our perpetual involuntary singlehood. Trust me, if you are waiting for Black Prince Charming to come riding in on a horse so you can marry him and have a bunch of beautiful black babies, know that time is not on your side. Don't believe me? How about Oprah Winfrey? On her talk show, which is now repurposed on her OWN cable network, a very attractive 27-year-old African American woman said her friends were waiting on their one true "black love." Oprah paused, blinked, and replied with complete seriousness: "You know what those [friends] are going to be doing? Waiting. Just look at the numbers. The numbers just aren't there!"

And here's why: Black women far excel above black men both educationally and professionally—with black girls outperforming their male counterparts as early as elementary school, according to Stanford law professor Ralph Richard Banks, author of *Is Marriage for White People: How the African American Marriage Decline Affects Everyone*. By the time black women get to college, they vastly outnumber black men, with more than 1,400,000 black women but fewer than 900,000 black men. In postgraduate education the divide is even greater, with black women earning higher degrees over black men more than two to one.

The most relevant aspect of this numbers game, says Banks, is the overwhelming rate in which African American men are incarcerated. Of the over two million people in the United States who are in jail or in prison, 40 percent, more than 840,000 are African Americans, with one in ten black men in their early thirties behind bars. "For men in their early twenties, the incarceration rate is closer to one in eight," writes Banks.

He further points out that black women are three times as likely as white women never to live with an intimate partner.

And biologically speaking, women have roughly until the age of thirty-five to safely conceive children without risk and/or medical intervention. A man can pump out sperm until he draws his last breath. So with time ever so unfairly not on our side, the 5 percent of marriageable black men know they're a hot commodity.

And so are you.

But first we need to free your mind of all the misguided assumptions, stereotypes, and deep-seated fears and/or hostilities you might have about looking past the brothers and to someone less familiar. A few attitude adjustments will help you finally see the potential in others and get the love you long for.

Assumption #1: *There is no black man shortage. My friend is married to a good, hardworking black man. My father and brother are both great, too.*

Attitude Adjustment: Even though some black women are happily married to their black counterparts doesn't mean the same applies for all. The idea that: "She got hers; if I just do what she did, I could have mine too!" is ludicrous. But there are some of you who, when anything suggests to the contrary, answer back with tightly shut eyes, thumbs pressed against the ears, and a loud, repetitive "La-la-la!" Grow up, ladies! Proclaiming that every black woman can find her black mate if she just did x-y-z is a very counterproductive and immature way of thinking. What works for others may not often work for you. Plus, the data don't lie. Denying that there is a shortage is tantamount to believing the world is flat. So unless you're planning to marry your friend's husband, your father, or your brother, be open-minded about the other possibilities.

Assumption #2: *I don't want to be some man's jungle fever fantasy.*

Attitude Adjustment: Okay, so there are some white men who may be curious about what it would be like to be with a black woman. There are some black women who are curious about Asian men. There's nothing wrong with being interested in someone who is different from what you're used to, nor is it wrong to be physically aroused by those differences. The reality is that most men who are serious about building a relationship love and appreciate you for more than what's on the outside. Need evidence? More and more of *them* are marrying us. In 2000, 95,000 black women were married interracially. By 2006, those numbers rose to 117,000. Of course, when you're just starting out a little discernment doesn't hurt. We'll talk more about this later.

Assumption #3: *I like to go to the club, and black men are the best dancers.*

Attitude Adjustment: I'll admit it. My white husband of eight years is rhythmically challenged. Why not let your suitor's lack of steppin' skills inspire you to bond in a dance class? Ever learn how to salsa? Tango? Everyone in the class will be there to learn, so that keeps the pressure off. Sure, there may be some truth to the joke about white people hearing extra beats that don't exist, but I've known plenty of black guys who didn't know how to move to a groove. I'm willing to bet you do, too.

Assumption #4: *I could never take him to church with me.*

Attitude Adjustment: This situation requires some serious introspection on your part. If "all are welcome" means only all those whose skin is chocolate brown, then it might be time to seriously rethink what kind of church you're attending. Remember that song we learned as kids, "Jesus Loves the Little Children"? As I recall, the Lord's got love for red, yellow, black, and white. Deborrah Cooper, life coach, dating expert, online radio host, and author of *Sucka Free Love: How to Avoid Dating The Dumb, The Deceit-*

ful, The Dastardly, The Dysfunctional & The Deranged!, places the majority of the blame for black women being perpetually single on black churches. Black women, she says, are being conditioned to wait *ad nauseam* for God to bring their black man, and that we shouldn't have too many expectations of his accomplishments and goals—or lack thereof. "He could be a bum on the street with no teeth. If he's a godly man, you should be happy with the *blessing*." Considering the Bible calls us to be *equally* yoked, I'm going to go out on a limb and assume He'd want you to at least find someone with a job and a good set of chompers.

Assumption #5: *Dating interracially means I'm disloyal to my race.*

Attitude Adjustment: Every time I hear this argument I often wonder why, for so many years, black men have had a pass on dating and marrying interracially. That outrage was so 1980s. Today, it is accepted—and almost expected—that an accomplished black man will leave his community and marry a woman who is *not* black, if he gets married at all. "A black man who earns more than a hundred thousand dollars per year is less likely to have ever married than a black man who earns seventy-five thousand dollars a year," says Banks. And what's more, "The highest-earning black men are more than twice as likely as their white counterparts never to have married."

And while there are black women who may not like it, the level of outrage is not nearly as equal when a black woman follows suit. There is a pressure for us to be *down* with our brothers, to love and protect them, despite their statistical inability to protect and nurture *us*—to marry *us* and be fathers to *our* children.

Loyalty goes both ways, ladies. Don't miss an opportunity to find the love of your life because you're scared of what someone who doesn't *want* you thinks of you.

Assumption #6: *White people smell funny when they get wet.*

Attitude Adjustment: I kid you not, this was a *real* comment from a *real* black woman who is resistant to dating outside her race. Even if this is your honest impression, white men aren't walking around dripping wet unless they're lifeguards—in which case, the hot and manly look of the typical lifeguard will overshadow the perceived wet-puppy odor.

In truth I can somewhat identify with the fact that certain races who adhere to a diet different from what I'm used to can give off a distinct smell. I remember an Indian girl I sat next to in grade school who always smelled like hot dogs to me. I would think to myself, *It's eight a.m.—who eats hot dogs for breakfast?* When I was old enough to know better, I realized that hot dog smell was curry. Now, I could delve deeper and get into the biology of body odors and how diet and hormones affect someone's smell, but that's a science lesson I won't be dealing with in this book. Plus, I know a few black women who always smell like burnt hair—so there.

Assumption #7: *I just don't think I'll have anything in common with someone who is not black.*

Attitude Adjustment: My husband and I were raised on opposite sides of the country. I was solid middle class and my father was a garbage collector with an eighth-grade education. My husband's father is a judge, both his siblings went to Ivy League schools, and he followed after his dad and went to Boston College. The family had a vacation home in St. Martin, while we took summer road trips to Yosemite in our two-tone-blue bubble-top van. But despite our backgrounds, we realized we were both homebodies with a love of culinary arts, home improvement projects, and toiling in the garden. We had a strong sense of family, shared similar political views, and had lively and spirited debates on the points where we disagreed.

Here's a challenge for you: make a list of all the things you like to do. Take note of what your passions are, your goals and your dreams. Then close your eyes and consider for a moment whether any of those goals and dreams are exclusive to black people?

If you give it a chance, you'd be surprised at what you might actually have in common with someone who has had a different life experience, and you might be delighted at what you will learn about yourself. I recall once early in our relationship, my husband took me to my first-ever dining experience at a five-star restaurant. I had honestly never seen so many glasses, plates, various sizes of forks, knives, and spoons prepared for only two people in my entire life! "Work from the outside in," he gently whispered in my ear, and then he kissed me on the cheek and pulled out my chair. It was *My Fair Lady*, Christelyn-style.

Assumption 8: *African American culture is the most comfortable to me. It's what I'm used to.*

Attitude Adjustment: In her relationship column on examiner.com, Cooper fielded a question from a successful black woman who was living and dating a Japanese man who often discussed marriage. The woman, who mentioned she had been raised in an inner-city housing project in Northern California, felt that "something was missing" in the relationship because of cultural differences and her "previous experiences with black men." She was so overwrought with confusion that she was considering a breakup with her Asian beau. To which Cooper replied (and I'll admit I *loved* this):

> You have in your hands and arms a man who loves you, who treats you like you are special and unique and precious. You have in your hands a man who wants to be with you for the rest of his life, who will honor and respect and adore you. Yet you write me whining about some nonsense that you "are used to" which evidently didn't get you anywhere. Right? Because you sure didn't mention how any of those BLACK men treated you like you were a queen!
>
> Girlfriend, life is about changing. A young lady who had the gumption and skill set to get her butt out of the projects of Bayview/Hunter's Point and onto the fast track of academic success via international studies and a graduate degree from Oxford University is special indeed. Why you are wasting your time focusing on the past and longing for someone who has a similar upbringing is beyond my understanding.

'Tis all I need to say about that.

Assumption #9: *I'm afraid of a* Guess Who's Coming to Dinner *moment.*

Attitude Adjustment: On this, I can truly empathize. The day my husband introduced me to his family would have been horrifying for me, if only I had been there. His family lives on the East Coast and we lived in California. During a family vacation, my future husband decided to pass my picture around the dinner table, which would have been fine, except his family had no idea I was black. According to my sister-in-law, the reaction ranged from disbelief to surprise—and from my future father-in-law, downright panic.

"Mike talked about you all the time, but he was always so vague, and we could never figure out why. But as soon as I saw the picture, that explained it all!" recalls my sister-in-law.

As things progress in your relationship, the *Guess Who's Coming to Dinner* moment will be inevitable, and your friend and family reactions to your interracial/intercultural relationship will vary from "Meh—what's the big deal?" to Mom and Dad reaching for the really good booze. It's best to prep your family well in advance, says Tina B. Tessina, PhD (aka Dr. Romance), psychotherapist and author of *The Unofficial Guide to Dating Again.* "Don't set this new person up to experience rejection, or a family disaster. If there's an issue, let your date know what the problems are, and if there are any real trigger issues to stay away from. (More on this issue in chapter 15, where we discuss the do's and don'ts of prepping for the first family meeting.)

Assumption #10: *I had this picture in my head about who and what my husband would look like. In my mind, he was tall, handsome, and chocolate. I just can't picture myself with anybody else.*

Attitude Adjustment: There's nothing wrong with wishing to marry your dream black man. You are entitled to that. But what if he never comes? What's the contingency plan? What will you do if you've wasted the fifteen to twenty years of your youth and fertility waiting for, trying to change for someone who didn't, couldn't, and wouldn't ever be what you wanted or needed him to be?

Even as a child I had always wanted to be married. Before I met my husband, it had never occurred to me that I wouldn't marry someone black. You marry your kind: That's just the way it is for most people. I met the father of my oldest child, who is black, in college. He dangled that marriage carrot over my head throughout our relationship, so it was pretty natural for me to assume that when I told him I was unexpectedly pregnant, a quickie marriage was on the table. To my shock and deep, deep sadness, he outright refused to marry me. (I would later discover that he would talk marriage to all his future girlfriends—that's how he keeps them around for so long.)

In the end, my dream marriage to that black man blew away in the exhaust of a U-Haul as my daughter and I moved back home to live with my parents. I had just made the biggest misstep of my life thus far. Yes, I got a beautiful, sweet, brilliant daughter. But she would forever have to deal with the confusion of mismatched surnames, ping-ponging back a forth for visits with her father, and always, always, no matter what, wishing she lived in the same house with *both* of her biological parents, despite a true and honest love for her stepfather.

It took a lot of shame and loss for me to learn that, ultimately, the values a potential mate possessed were of the utmost importance. The color of the man was irrelevant. This was my Plan B. But it should have been plan Numero Uno from the very beginning.

And now, just for fun, I thought I'd add some of the *craziest* reasons some of the women on my blog have heard for why they should *not* date a rainbeau.

Laugh because it's hilarious; cry because it's true.

My great aunt's response to my engagement [to a white man] was something like, *"Don't come cryin' to me when he kills you. White men don't know how to leave like black men."*

This was a real statement that I heard from a woman regarding why she won't date interculturally. She said that she can't date an African man because, *"All of them have three or more wives, and besides, I ain't running round in the jungle with my hair all nappy trying to avoid lions and tigers and bears."*

Other responses I've heard:

"Nope, can't date a rainbow man because I want to win that electric slide contest down at the club, and he will just mess me up!"

"I can't date a white guy because he would laugh at my nappy pubic hair."

"What y'all going to do when the race war begins?"

"I can't date a white man because, 'it's' pink."

"I couldn't marry an Asian man because they eat too much rice."

CHAPTER TWO

Janice

Who's Swirling?

The people I surround myself with now all date interracially; they're not stuck on any kind of ideas about who people should be dating. I think it is the new norm.

—DANIELLE MILTON, CPA, TWENTY-EIGHT

Black and white swirls are just the tip of the iceberg as inter-ethnic and interfaith mixing continue to rise.

The headlines are encouraging: Mixed families are on the rise, and spawning a whole new generation of crosscultural and mixed-race kids. While no one can really say for sure how the growth of a multiracial population will change the country, most assuredly black women should take heart that as the American melting pot may one day resemble more of a gumbo of wonderfully blended racial and cultural influences—all in one family—that we can begin partaking in this tasty trend.

"Everyone is reaching toward love," says Latoya Peterson, owner and editor of the online site Racialicious. "Everyone wants to be understood and everyone wants to be respected for who they are, everyone wants to be found attractive or beautiful, and that their race has not already spoken for them, and that's constant across the board, even for white people. You don't want your race to speak for you in dating, and yet I feel like there's that cultural fear that stems from talking about race, is why we can't have productive conversations about interracial relationships without falling back into stereotypes, fetishes, and ridiculousness."

While the rates of intermarriage vary widely depending on gender, race, and ethnicity, data from the 2009 Census Bureau finds gender differences are most pronounced among blacks and Asians: Black men tend to marry outside their racial group twice as often as black women do, while among Asians, it's women who are more likely to marry someone from a different group. Black Hispanics and American Indians have the overall highest rates of intermarriage, with black Hispanic men choosing black women in greater numbers while American Indian men choosing white women in greater numbers than women of their own group.

But this is still progress ... right?

"*Whew!* That's a loaded question," laughs Peterson, "I believe there is more progress, not as much as we would have hoped when you look at when the Loving decision came through (the 1967 landmark civil right case ending race-based restrictions on marriage), and you look at how much we've progressed and how little we've progressed at the same time. It's kind of ridiculous, because now interracial couples are not unusual, there's not the same knee-jerk reaction in most circles. There might be distrust, there still might be problems, there might be people overriding their experiences onto this couple—like the interracial hate stare, which we joke about on the site—and unfortunately it still happens because someone is drawing up conclusions about your relationship surfaces based on what they think."

The idea that we've become a postracial America is a bunch of media malarkey. Race still matters in this country, and the reasons why African American women don't mix interracially are varied. Even so, that doesn't have to stop you from getting your swirl on.

Making the Connection

> *At the end of the day, people have more in common*
> *than they don't . . . if the only thing we're talking about*
> *is color then let's look at what we have in common.*
> —LINDA LOCKHART, JOURNALIST, FIFTY-NINE

Of the mixed couples we interviewed for the book, and the throngs who frequently comment on the Beyond Black & White blog, the thing that brought them together, and keeps them connected, involves shared interest. But even getting people of diverse backgrounds together in the first place, sociologists say, can still be challenging. Despite the burgeoning diversity, even people in large cities, including my own beloved hometown of

Los Angeles, are largely segregated by community. Where I live in the southwest region of the city, you can count the number of white families living in my little upscale urban African American circle on one hand. It is changing, but by no means quickly.

On a national level, Bill Rankin's mapping project, originally published in the spring 2010 issue of *Perspecta*, the journal of the Yale School of Architecture, illustrates this point in living color. Based on data from the 2009 Census, Rankin's map is able to show how Chicago, a city with a long history of segregation and failed public housing initiatives that began with the development of racially delineated "community areas" in the 1920s, still has those same "perfectly homogeneous neighborhoods" today.

"It's fascinating that we're very segregated where we live, and we're still segregated in the workforce," says Racialicious's Peterson. "We aren't having as much contact with each other as we would expect to be such a diverse nation. And where there isn't a wiliness to challenge ingrained stereotypes or cultural stereotypes that we might have learned from the media or pop culture, that's where you get into these very strange ideas about other people."

Social distance, the theory that ascribes social class, race, and ethnicity or sexuality to the reasons different groups don't mix, concludes that whites and blacks are the most distant on the social scale, with Asians, Latinos, and American Indians in between, and are thus less likely to mingle and mix socially. That would give credence for why white men and black women are more likely, according to statistics, to partner with someone within their own race in larger numbers than any other gender or racial group.

But look closely and you will see a gigantic fly in the ointment on that argument, considering black men have a fairly high rate of interracial dating and marriage with the highest percentage according to the 2009 Census stats of couplings with white women. Even the class factor doesn't hold up in this equation, especially when you take into account the number of athletes and entertainers who date out—but don't have college degrees. (Hmmm . . . maybe money *can* buy you love.)

So as the world swirls, black women are stuck in lives filled with made-for-soap-opera drama and settling for less than they deserve. It is telling when a woman with her master's degree and making a decent amount of money decides to steal a car with her man just to prove she loves him, or a Christian woman and mother of four opts to marry a man serving a three-strikes sentence in prison because she doesn't want to be alone anymore, or the endless stories I have heard of women in adulterous relationships just so they could say they have got a black man, even though it's another woman's husband—and all because black women fear cultural isolation from their own community when they mix, date, and marry, says Atlanta psychotherapist and relationship expert Joyce Morely.

"The church, every Sunday, spews across the pulpit certain things that bring shame and guilt to the black woman," she says, "and that's why you have black women who stay in abusive situations just to stay together with black men, and you have the man getting what he wants and getting what he can and he's surviving while you have these women left feeling ashamed and with a lot of guilt. So are you willing to take *that* risk? There's risk with anybody that you meet."

Says Jennifer,* forty-four, who lives with her husband, Robert, fifty-eight, who is white, and their seven-year-old daughter in Fairfax, California, "I'm always interested when people comment that I'm ruining the African American family," she says. "Because there are a lot of African American families that are not two-parent family units, and the divorce rate among African Americans is higher than the national average [the divorce rate among African American couples is 70 percent, with 72 percent of African American children born to unwed mothers according to governmental statistics]. Until they can deal with that, I think they need to leave the rest of us alone."

I decided to chat about this with my second cousin, Monique Neal, a thirty-nine-year-old paralegal. She met Barry, a forty-five-year-old white elevator technician, ten years ago through an ad she placed on the website for the television series *Blind Date*. They live in Chino with their fast-growing toddler, Jada Rose Marie. Both had dated out before prior to their meeting. "The thing that I don't get is how my marriage is a betrayal. To who?" she vehemently questions. "How is it that I can find somebody to love and that's wrong? We laugh about it—even when they stare. Barry says, 'Take a picture it'll last longer.' I mean, what is the big deal?"

I mean, seriously! Even modern social lexicon is adapting to the change. Nowadays it's not uncommon to meet people proudly referring to themselves by monikers such as "blasian" (those of black and Asian ancestry), while still so many of us are singing loud and proud about "brown skin up against my brown skin"—and no offense to India.Arie, 'cause I actually love that song—when my brown skin swirling against white or tan is equally lovely when with a compatible partner.

But the reason behind it is simple—and yet so complex.

In many African social systems, much like the African American system, it is the woman who holds together the family and cultural ties to the community. She passes down the oral traditions, she passes down the food traditions (by the way, thanks for that, Mom), she passes down the religious traditions: She is everything. It is not that dissimilar from the matrilineal system among Jews.

It's the woman thing that had a number of Conservative Jews raised all holy hell in the media about Chelsea Clinton, a Methodist, and Marc Mezvinsky, a Conservative Jew, believing such marriages further diluted Jewish culture in the United States—some even suggesting that the former First Daughter convert to Judaism.

Interfaith marriages like the Clinton-Mezvinsky union are also growing in the United States, and according to the Pew Forum on Religion and Public Life, 37 percent of couples in the United States in 2008 didn't share the same faith. Twenty percent of Protestants have married out, says the survey. Another from American Religious Identification Survey in 2001 found the intermarriage rate was 39 percent for Muslims, 27 percent for Jews, 23 percent for Catholics, and 12 percent for Mormons—and many have found it to be quite heavenly being married to someone outside their faith while maintaining their own religious and cultural traditions.

Not that this is just a Jewish issue. There are plenty of right-leaning Christians who are not too thrilled about the trend either.

In an article in *USA Today,* published at the time of this blessed bifaith union, one pastor said he would not officiate a wedding between a Christian and a nonbeliever because of the increased difficulties that can arise for people who "hold their faith firmly and strongly. . . . The idea of absolute truth is what is at stake here."

The Truth Is Out There

What's at stake for African Americans, say objectors to the multicultural movement, is the very existence of African American culture.

Well, guess what? Not only is that the stinkiest load of sexist, misogynistic crapola, it's also not true. In the same way that my Jewish girlfriends who've chosen to marry someone of another faith still raise their children to be Jewish, so too, in many cases, black women involved in mixed-race and ethnic relationships say they feel more connected to their African American-ness.

"The more that I spent around boyfriends of other cultures,

the more I felt that I was a black woman," says thirty-four-year-old anthropologist/web designer Nicole Elgh, who's been swirling since her second grade crush on the little Mexican boy at her Catholic grammar school. Her husband of three years, Mathias Elgh, thirty-six, is a machinist from Stockholm, Sweden, where the two currently reside. She's Buddhist and he's an atheist. "And I feel like, when I have a child, I believe it would be to that child's advantage to have the option of being identified as black whether anyone else sees it or not. I want to provide that option to say that this is a culture that your mother grew up in and that you have the option to join."

"Since they're going to be part black, I know Nicole feels strongly about her culture and she wants to have a room dedicated to black things and black culture in our home, and I'm fine with that because that's going to be part of what they are," Mathias says. "It is an openness and an encouragement to find what will work for us."

Robert* in Fairfax adds: "I've always been appreciative and sensitive to minorities and their difficult lot in life," he says. "Not that I could ever genuinely identify with it, but maybe being in Jennifer's world helps me gain a greater appreciation and sensitivity of what it's like to be black or someone of a minority group in the United States."

"Sometimes I'll say to Linda: Let's go down to downtown Kirkwood and wave the flag," says journalist Steve Korris, fifty-nine, of the multiracial banner he and his wife, journalist Linda Lockhart, have been waving for thirty years. The couple, who live in St. Louis, have been true champions of interracial couplings and appeared in Ebony magazine in 1985 and on daytime talk shows, such as *The Sally Jessy Raphael Show*, touting the blessings of their mixed-race family. "We have relentlessly promoted what we do. We celebrate it, we announce it." Adds Linda: "To look at my life now and see some thirty years later and look at young couples and see that we're the old heads, it's so cool because they look like my family!"

Today, those opposed to mixed-raced unions like Linda's are in the minority. Results of the latest *USA Today*/Gallup poll revealed that Americans are approaching unanimity in their views of marriages between blacks and whites with a whopping 86 percent now approving of such unions. Americans' views, in general, on interracial marriage have undergone a major transformation in the past five decades. When Gallup first asked about black-white marriages in 1958, only 4 percent were on board with the swirl, and approval did not exceed the majority level until 1997. The results, based on surveys conducted between August 4 and 7, 2011, included an oversample of blacks.

The study concludes that this increase in approval of black-white marriage among all Americans is a likely result of changing attitudes within the population rather than changes in the composition of the population, with more socially progressive younger adults replacing less progressive older ones. And this trend mimics the growing support for gay marriage—although Americans are still less likely to accept that practice than interracial marriage. It also follows the trend toward increasing racial tolerance on other measures such as voting for a black (although we all know the man is biracial) president and an increasing belief in progress and equality for blacks in the United States more generally.

Call me crazy, and I have heard it before, but wasn't that what the whole civil rights movement rumble was all about: equality, justice, and our little piece of that life, liberty, and pursuit of happiness deal? To be judged by the content of one's character rather than by religion, ethnicity, or skin color, to choose without hindrance or restraint? It is the very definition of freedom.

"We're so afraid of tomorrow that we don't live in today," says Morely of Atlanta. "But that is part of our culturalization. There's a lot of stuff that we hold on to, and so we've got to learn how to let stuff go, and not keep believing all this stuff and letting people fill us with shame and guilt, to invalidate and not approve of us. If we can do it for ourselves, then it makes it a lot easier for us to take the risks we need to take."

"Black women need more than color connections," says, Kimberly*, a thirty-four-year-old stay-at-home Maryland mother of two whose husband, Jonathan, is of Polish and German descent. The couple, married five years, met on eHarmony. "For me, it was just another method of meeting men. It would not have mattered if I'd met him accidentally at the grocery store: At the end of the day I just wanted to find a really nice guy and if you have a really busy lifestyle, how else are you going to meet men?"

Says Danielle Milton, a twenty-eight-year old single African American auditor living in Kansas City, Missouri: "As I get older, among the people I interact with I'm finding my preferences are changing in terms of who I find attractive," Danielle says, adding, "I am so sick of these forums about why black women can't find love, and oh it's such a crisis for black women, and oh why aren't black men interested in black women—like that conversation has been going on since probably the time I was getting out of high school, so for ten years everyone's been bemoaning why they cannot find black men, and at this point it's come down to: accept being single and be cool with it or date interracially. It's stupid to shun what could be a meaningful relationship because of race. I'm so over this. It's time to move on."

The paltry number of eligible African American men is frightening—and it's real. So, ladies, it's time to get real if you're interested in finding a partner, a husband . . . or heck, if you just want to date more than a couple of times a year. Who we find attractive has a lot to do with whom we are exposed to, and if you haven't been around people of other races and cultures, either in school or at work or in your communities, it's a little harder to know what it is you find appealing about someone who doesn't look like you.

> If you haven't been around people of other races and cultures, it's a little harder to know what it is you find appealing about someone who doesn't look like you.

But divorcing ourselves from what we have always known is easier said than done. If it were, there would obviously be no need for this particular how-to manual. But thankfully black women are beginning to talk more about dating out, and about the complexities of our own sexuality at a time when the number of newscasts, articles, and blogs on the subject is ever increasing. It is, in fact, the issue that has captivated our cultural zeitgeist in the new millennium.

"There has been a lot of focus on black women and marriage, and black women's suitability for marriage," says Courtney Young, a pop culture writer in New York whose work has appeared in *The Nation,* Huffington Post, and *Ms.* "I think there's sort of this perverse reaction to Michelle Obama in the media that's propelling, at least in small part, this obsession with black women not being able to get married and not being able to find a suitable partner."

What she found in her studies is not dissimilar to what Christelyn and I have heard: a whole lotta yada-yada about how black women prefer only to date black men. "But that plays also into the way we talk about interracial couples," Young continues, "and I think that the way we talk about interracial couples, and black women in interracial relationships, as being a way that goes against racism can be a double-edged sword, in that being able to love whoever you choose to love is always a step in the right direction, and it's progress. But *racism* is a bit more complicated than that."

To illustrate the point, Young points to the well-publicized incident in which actress Halle Berry, who, during a custody battle with her former beau, and father of her daughter, Gabriel Aubry, accused the French Canadian model of having called her a "nigger" several times. While there were those who believed the Academy Award–winner made up the story to create sympathy, others were betting money on the ponies that he did, believing that no matter how many times a white man tells a black woman that he loves her, deep down he only sees the house negress.

New York psychologist Lisa Orbe-Austin, PhD, in her dissertation on interracial and interethnic dating and mating, found that racist people can indeed be interracially dating or interracially married. "There is an idea in the cultural mores that someone dates interracially and that makes them nonracist. Like you often hear a white man say, 'Well I dated a black woman,' as if that now takes them off the hook for any kind of racial issue. But I did find in my research that people who do have racist ideas and notions and identities were married, but they tended to be unsatisfied in those relationships, obviously, and the people of color who were in these relationships with them tended to have very fragmented identities too; they didn't have a good sense of their own racial identity either."

Halle's plight (or performance, depending on what side of the aisle you're on) explains the angst many black women feel about submitting their passions to a man of another hue, particularly a white man. And while being cautious can certainly protect you from getting hurt by the wrong guy, fear is irrational, dysfunctional, and debilitating, and can keep you away from your Mr. Right One.

So, here is your assignment, if you choose to accept it: expose yourself to more men. (And I mean in a with-your-clothes-on kind of way.) Meeting more of *them* and learning about them actually puts you more in touch with *you* and increases the likelihood that what you find in a "rainbeau" man goes beyond his physicality. Twenty years from now that hot black dude who has been cheating on you left and right isn't going to look so good—deeper connections are what maintains a relationship for the long haul.

"One thing I've realized is that I am much more comfortable with who I am and that race really shouldn't be such a big deal," Jennifer says, noting that being in an interracial marriage has made her more understanding of other minority groups. "There are a lot of African Americans who are against gay marriage, and it wasn't that long ago that African Americans weren't allowed to be married, and they weren't allowed to be married to anybody of another color. We had to fight for our rights to be married to who we wanted. Shouldn't everybody else have that same right?"

After all, she says, despite whatever differences we may have, we're all pretty much the same under the skin: "You just have to look for it—and if you're willing to look for it, it's definitely there," she says.

"I have met black women who were not happy about their dating situation," Jennifer adds. "And I'm meeting women who are attractive, educated, they have everything going for them, but they can't meet anybody to date. You could sit around and wait hoping that you'll find someone that's the same race, the same religion? Do you really want to do that when you can find somebody who will make you happy who is of another race or religion?"

That you are reading this book, I'm guessing the answer is no.

What is wonderful about what is happening now is that mixed partnerships mean more than just white guys: it's Asian, Persian, Latino, Native American; Hindu, Muslim, Buddhist . . . the swirls are endless. And there's so much support out there for those dating and marrying out. Mixed-race groups are popping up all over college campuses, social media and dating sites, and conferences. There are even multiracial film festivals—all positive signs that you're not alone if you decide to step outside your color and culture box. Once you start really exploring your options, who knows? You might end up with that a black guy who has been hiding out on the other side of town you used to never go to. The point is, why limit yourself just to one group—it's not like everyone else is.

CHAPTER THREE

Janice

Best U. S. Cities That Swirl

Southern California, with all its liberal ideals and live-and-let-live attitude, is a great place for interracial and intercultural couples to thrive. The Bay Area and Pacific Northwest are perpetually on the top of any list that tracks this sort of data—and my hometown, the wonderfully swirling City of Angels, is usually in the mix, too. (I love L.A.!)

If you're looking for an interracial coupling, it's probably best to keep your booty out of Tempe, Arizona; Fayetteville, Arkansas; Albany, Georgia; Detroit, Michigan; and Sparta, Wisconsin. But did you know Denver, Colorado, and Minneapolis, Minnesota, are also hubs where mixed couples and their families flourish? Are you game for an international swirl? Top picks include Paris, London, and Vancouver, where interracial marriages are twice the national average, according to the 2006 Canadian Census. Based on responses from readers of Beyond Black & White and the most recent poll by *Interrace Magazine,* which has been surveying its readers on the subject for more than a decade, we compiled this list of a dozen U.S. cities for those of you still in the market for a mate—or couples looking to move away from unwelcoming eyes. Can't afford to move? Well, maybe it's time you took an extended exploratory trip. (You know you're so due for a vacation anyway.)

Minneapolis, Minnesota

The Twin Cities are not only one of the friendliest places for interracial couples, they're also one of the fittest. Ranked third in each of two new national surveys—one on physical fitness and one on quality of life—the Minneapolis metropolitan area metro area boasts a high number of people who are involved in regular physical activity or exercise as well as those in excellent or very good health. For those of you job hunting, Minneapolis has a low unemployment rate and loads of available parkland, recreation centers, and physical education classes. And with ready access to golf courses, bike and walking paths, park facilities, and dog parks, it makes for a great place for living with a mate—and finding one.

San Diego, California

At the southernmost tip of the Golden State, San Diego is a city that believes in community as a vital part of one's quality of life in the region. Continuing its move toward a Clean Generation, the city provides programs offering financial incentives for renewable energy as well as energy efficiency and water conservation improvements by its residents. Already a national leader in solar energy, San Diego's "green" home improvements will not only have the potential to save money for countless home owners, they will create jobs for those who live there. It's a win-win for those who are looking for little economic stability in a city and environmental consciousness to go along with their swirl.

Montclair, New Jersey

A township in Essex County, New Jersey, Montclair is the fiftieth largest municipality in the state by population and attracts many who work for major media organizations in New York City, including the *New York Times* and *Newsweek*, according to a March 11, 2007, posting from Gawker.com. It is also home to many commuters to New York City and the metro area. Open to an interfaith relationship? Proportionally, there are more Muslims, Jews, and Catholics in Montclair than the country's average. On a national level, Montclair leans strongly toward the Democratic Party, and in 2008, Barack Obama received 83 percent of the vote here. Montclair boasts a plethora of art institutions and theaters, and despite its relatively small size has many art venues. But before you make a move, make sure your bank account can handle it. The median price for a house in Montclair is $670,400, which is more than three times the national average, and the cost of living is more than 48 percent higher than the U.S. average.

San Jose, California

The city's website features a tab boasting San Jose's cultural and ethnic diversity and the rich cultural identity of its many neighborhoods. Residents speak more than fifty-two different languages, and the city sponsors numerous cultural festivals, with many ethnic chambers of commerce active throughout the community. San Jose is the largest city in the Bay Area, located roughly fifty miles south of San Francisco and 390 miles north of Los Angeles and is the third largest city in California, following L.A. and San Diego according to a 2011 survey from the California Department of Finance. At the heart of this dynamic region is a thriving economy sustained in part by many high-tech and manufacturing companies, bringing in a high percentage of foreign-born residents—39 percent of the population who live in the city include high-tech workers from both East and South Asia, as well as Eastern European immigrants and poorer immigrants from Latin America, many of whom can be found in the large, multigenerational barrio, the Alum Rock district. San Jose also has the largest Vietnamese population of any city in the world outside Vietnam.

Denver, Colorado

Situated due east of the majestic Rocky Mountains, the Mile-High City of Denver is the most populous city in the state with eighty official neighborhoods, most all of them featuring parks or other community focal points. Denver has also enjoyed success as a pioneer in the fast-casual restaurant industry, with many popular national chain restaurants founded and based in Denver. Chipotle Mexican Grill, Quizno's, and Smashburger were founded and are headquartered here. A 2011 study by Walk Score ranked Denver as the sixteenth most walkable of the fifty largest U.S. cities—and you'll need places to stroll with your rainbeau after one of those monster-size Chipotle burritos. (Or, better yet, just share one.)

⚬

Washington, D.C.

With a majority African American population, Chocolate City's unique history is shaped by this strong African American heritage, and yet it has one of the most diverse ethnic populations in the country with a cadre of foreign delegations from the countries of the world flocking to this cosmopolitan city. Notably, the city boasts a growing Latino population representing people from every Central and South American country, with a particularly large El Salvadoran community. There is also an emergent Ethiopian population. While D.C. lost residents to surrounding suburbs in the nineties, new housing and urban revitalization is now attracting people back to the city for a downtown renaissance of housing, offices, entertainment, and nightlife. The majority of residents hold bachelor's degrees or higher, compared to the 27 percent of the U.S. population, and the median age is thirty-five. "Neither northern nor southern, sometimes urban, sometimes country and often soulful," as the city's site declares, D.C. is a place where gay, lesbian, bisexual, and transgender communities also thrive.

⁓

Seattle, Washington

The birthplace of Jimi Hendrix and home to grunge rock and heavy coffee drinking, Seattle is also a hotbed of "green technologies." Researchers at Central Connecticut State University consistently rank Seattle and Minneapolis as the two most literate cities among America's largest cities, and additionally, data from the Census Bureau indicate that Seattle has a higher percentage of college graduates than any other major American city, with approximately 53 percent of its residents aged twenty-five and older holding a bachelor's degree or higher. The Emerald City has seen a major increase in immigration in recent decades; the foreign-born population increased 40 percent between the 1990 and 2000 censuses. The Seattle area is also home to a large Vietnamese population. In addition, the Seattle area is home to more than thirty thousand Somali immigrants.

⁓

Oakland, California

Considering itself "a model city," Oakland's racial makeup is one of the country's most diverse. A cosmopolitan city with friendly, distinct neighborhoods, Oakland produces a gumbo of cultures, arts, music, politics, languages, and cuisines with international impact. The many parks and scenic views of the Bay and open space, along with thriving neighborhoods, affordable housing, access to services, and superior cultural and recreational amenities makes Oakland one of the most desirable and livable cities in the East Bay. The twentieth-century influx of immigrants from around the globe, along with thousands of African American war-industry workers who relocated from the Deep South during the 1940s, is how Oakland became one of the most ethnically diverse major cities in the country. Oakland is known for its history of political activism, as well as its professional sports franchises and major corporations, which include health care and , as well as manufacturers of household products. The city is a transportation hub for the greater Bay Area, and its shipping port is the fifth busiest in the United States.

Columbus, Ohio

The state's capital and one of the third largest cities in the American Midwest has both a diverse population and economy, based on education, government, insurance, banking, fashion, defense, aviation, food, clothes, logistics, steel, energy, medical research, health care, hospitality, retail, and technology. In 2011, the city had five corporations named to the U.S. Fortune 500 list including Nationwide Mutual Insurance Company, American Electric Power, Limited Brands, Momentive Specialty

Chemicals, and Big Lots. Major foreign corporations operating or with divisions in the city include Germany-based Siemens and Roxane Laboratories; Finland-based Vaisala; Japan-based Techneglas, Inc., Tomasco Mulciber Inc., and A Y Manufacturing; and Switzerland-based ABB Group and Mettler Toledo. According to Census reports, the number of foreign-born residents accounted for eighty-two percent of the new residents in Columbus between 2000 and 2006.

San Antonio, Texas

In 2011, San Antonio was estimated to be the twenty-fourth largest metropolitan area in the United States with a population of 2.2 million, according to recent U.S. Census Bureau figures. San Antonio is the fourth fastest growing large city in the nation from 2000 to 2006, and the fifth fastest-growing from 2007 to 2008. San Antonio's diversity stems from its strong military presence—it is home to Fort Sam Houston, Lackland Airforce Base, Randolf Airforce Base, and Brooks City-Base, with Camp Bullis and Camp Stanley outside the city, and five Fortune 500 companies: Valero Energy Corp, Tesoro, USAA, Clear Channel Communications, and NuStar Energy. Other large companies that operate regional headquarters in the city include: Nationwide Mutual Insurance Company, Kohl's, Allstate, Chase Bank, Philips, Wells Fargo, Toyota, Medtronic, Sysco, Caterpillar Inc., AT&T, West Corporation, Citigroup, Boeing, QVC, and Lockheed Martin. So if you're looking for a job, as well as a mate, this might be a great place to set up stakes.

Rochester, New York

Ranked as the sixth most-livable city among three hundred and seventy nine U.S. metropolitan areas in the twenty-fifth edition (2007) of the *Places Rated Almanac*, Rochester also received the top ranking for overall quality of life among U.S. metro areas with populations of more than 1 million in a 2007 study by *Expansion Management* magazine. Rochester is an international center of higher education, including medical and technological development. The region is known for many acclaimed universities, and several of them are renowned for their research programs and home to corporations such as Kodak, Bausch & Lomb, and Xerox. It's home to a number of religious denominations, including Hindu, Islamic, and Bahai communities.

Honolulu, Hawaii

The thirteenth largest city in the nation sits in the middle of the Pacific Ocean and is where President Barack Obama once called home. It is a bastion of culture and art, be it in its museums and concert halls or the urban hubs that have been embraced by Hollywood's television and film communities. Hawaii's economic base is primarily tourism and the city uses its cultural and artistic diversity to draw visitors into their eclectic ethnic mix, which draws on Native Hawaiian traditions as well as the tremendous contributions of the Filipino, Chinese, Portuguese, Scottish, Greek, Okinawan, and Samoan communities. Considered one of the world's top ten most livable cities, Honolulu has fashioned its culture and arts and a leading factor in building "strong cities (and) strong families for a strong America," according to the city's website.

That, and it's a great place to get lei'd. (Okay, wickedly lame pun intended, but it still sounds like paradise to me.)

CHAPTER FOUR

Christelyn

Feel Like You Need Permission To Swirl? Girl, You Got It.

Forget for a moment about the statistics that say 70 percent of black women are single and that the pool of marriageable black men is drying out from a puddle. I won't even mention that 72 percent of black children are born outside of marriage. Let's forget about that for a while.

Let's focus on you.

You are not a statistic. And if you're reading this book, chances are you are the crème de la crème, looking for your very own Mr. Crème de la Crème. As women of color we are taught almost before birth that we are to "hold it down" at home, at work, and in our family relationships. It's been our responsibility since slavery to lie down and take so much mess and abuse:

We're told we're inferior, our hair is too nappy, and no one, even black men don't want us. Forget everything you've been told, because you've been hoodwinked, bamboozled, taken for a ride (both literally and figuratively), shafted, and snookered.

Black woman, you are beautiful. The way your natural hair coils from your head, your dark, almond-shaped eyes, high cheekbones, full lips, one hundred shades of brown, glorious smile, and voluptuous figure is uniquely yours.

So forget the horse excrement about nobody wanting you. Leave that mess about you being *too this* or *too that* or that no non-black man will ever want you. It's a lie. We are told the statistics are wrong, and that there's plenty of black men out there, but when you go to church, the club, work, or a party, you wonder what's wrong with you that you haven't found your Black Prince Charming yet. Meanwhile, are we supposed to ignore that black people have the lowest marriage rate in the country while having the highest out-of-wedlock rate? Let me get this straight: Marriage = unlikely. Baby out-of-wedlock = very likely. Are you okay with that?

Clearance #1: *Free yourself from the shackles of being a "sojourner." You are not a race traitor if you put your health and your happiness first.*

We're the only women in America who are praised for working as if slavery is still legal, while raising children virtually alone with no support, told by our parents, extended family, and friends that we need to get an education and support ourselves, not always out of self-actualization, but out of pure fear for our financial future. Our parents tell us to be self-sufficient, because there's a good chance you'll have to go life alone, meet someone long enough to procreate, then eventually said person goes *poof!* for a variety of reasons. We're also told that while we do everything, we should let our men lead, whether he works or not, is abusive or not, lazy or not, a cheater or not, and terrible businessman or not, or a babymama creator or not.

There's even a scientific name for it: Sojourner's Syndrome. According to researchers who conducted the 2009 Duke University study:

Despite improvements in many aspects of health, African American women experience early onset of disease and disability and increased mortality because of health disparities. African American women experience stress and health disadvantages because of the interaction and multiplicative effects of race, gender, class, and age. Sojourner Syndrome is an illustrative and symbolic representation that describes the multiple roles and social identities of African American women on the basis of historical referents and adaptive behaviors that fostered survival and resilience under oppressive circumstances. Adaptive behaviors also precipitated health risks due to chronic active coping. Weathering describes the cumulative health impact of persistent stress and chronic active coping that contributes to early health deterioration and increased morbidity, disability, and mortality in African American women. An emancipatory, knowing nursing perspective provides a viewpoint from which to examine social injustices that create conditions for the excessive health burdens experienced by African American women and to frame nursing actions that create opportunities to promote health and eliminate health disparities.

The Sojourner Syndrome, aka "The Black Woman's Burden," is not new. It has always been a matter of our very survival to take on so much. So many of us black women have given up on the idea about being happy, loved, respected, and, if we so choose, married with quality fathers for our children.

Why the "Strong Black Woman" Mentality Must Die

I once did a man-on-the-street interview with some very handsome rainbeaus at a blog conference in Los Angeles. The goal of the interviews were to gauge how nonblack men feel about dating and mating with black women. The good news? You'll be shocked to know they see black women as just that—women. And, know what? They like you. But one gorgeous thirtysomething guy told me that one issue that keeps many rainbeaus from stepping up is the myth of the strong black woman. The "Strong Black Woman" is capable of just about everything, from leaping tall buildings with a single bound and lifting cars with one hand to change a tire. Sure, it's nice to be considered more durable than a dandelion, but it sucks when men feel like there's little use for them outside of their phalluses. There's nothing wrong with being independent, but when the general impression people have of you is of some man-woman who scoffs at the very idea of falling back on a man, or if it's hurting your dating prospects then, the Strong Black Woman (SBW) must die. Lots of readers can attest to that:

"I do think that the SBW is a facade for many. . . . I feel like there's a big fear that no one is going to accept them any other way. AA women are supposed to be functional workhorses while other women have been allowed to be ornamental/decorative, cared for, pampered, et cetera," says one BB&W commenter who calls herself ForestElfQueen.

"The SBW label turns things that should be positive like education, wealth, worldly experiences, responsibility, loyalty and—most important—choice, into negative things. In combination in a black woman these things that are good are made bad. If you're brown-skinned, these things, which are very often good things, become a burden that negatively puts into question your womanhood and femininity," says iHeartLove.

You must empower yourself and understand that you don't have to passively wait for any old piece of man to show interest in you, then accept whatever scraps you get. And there is nothing, I repeat, nothing, wrong with choosing a mate who is financially capable of supporting you at least temporarily while you bear his children within wedlock. This does not make you weak!

Does the Black Community Need to Give You the Green Light to Swirl?

If so, I wouldn't hold your breath, because by and large, you are not going to get it. Because of a cluster-cuss of societal, behavioral, and institutional problems, the black community at large depends on the work, resources, and sacrifice of black women. This has been the case since slavery, so I doubt this structure is destined to change in our lifetimes. But if you want a chance to optimize your love relationships and expand your dating pool, then you're going to have to cross that invisible, self-imposed line in the sand that forbids you from seeking the best man for the job, regardless of race, color, or creed.

At some point, you may have to make a decision, like Luna, another avid BB&W reader, did. "My family can just keep yapping for all I care. I'm the one that's happy, and they're the ones who live the crisis du jour routine because of who they associate with, their past choices about education, their past choices about being single mothers, etc. I have no intention of being like them just to prove, to them, my solidarity with black people. Hah, that is never going to happen."

That may be harsh to read, but the bottom line is that Luna has made the decision to be happy with a significant other who doesn't meet the preferred-men-black-women-can-date-and-marry checklist, and she has no regrets.

Paul Carrick Brunson, founder of the coaching and match-making service One Degree from Me, stresses that women looking for a mate should be open to all their dating and mating possibilities and have high standards and "nonnegotiables." "Any mate who deliberately jeopardizes your health or your happiness are the only two nonnegotiables," he says. In other words, it's time to judge a mate for character above color. Paul is a black man, married to a black woman for a decade and they've just had a beautiful baby son.

Ralph Richard Banks, the Jackson Eli Reynolds Professor of Law at Stanford Law School, and author of *Is Marriage for White People?: How the African American Marriage Decline Affects Everyone,* said in an August 2011 piece in the *Wall Street Journal* that "Black women confront the worst relationship market of any group because of economic and cultural forces that are not of their own making; and they have needlessly worsened their situation by limiting themselves to black men. I also arrived at a startling conclusion: Black women can best promote black marriage by opening themselves to relationships with men of other races." Mr. Banks is also black.

Clearance #2: *You are allowed to love a rainbeau and still advocate for your people.*

The personal is not always the political.

I was once interviewed by a popular black radio host in Cincinnati, Ohio, who questioned my motivation to found and organize No Wedding No Womb, an initiative to raise awareness and find solutions to the out-of-wedlock epidemic in the black community. He asked me how I could advocate for a cause affecting black people, yet be married to a white man. My answer? Being married to someone who happens to be white does not make me any *less* black. I can still care and advocate for issues that affect my people (and my three daughters!) and not have to "prove" my dedication by my choice of mates. Did Harry Belafonte have to do that when he marched for civil rights while married to a white woman? Are advocates for the homeless required to marry the homeless to prove they really care? Do you have to be gay to stand up for same-sex unions? Exactly. Sometimes, the personal is *just* personal, and the political is *just* political. They can be separate. You can uplift your race and follow your bliss, and that doesn't make you a traitor.

No one would accuse Marian Wright Edelman, seventy-two, the founder of the Children's Defense Fund, of being a "sellout." To do so would almost be sacrilege. She was the first African American woman to be accepted into the Mississippi Bar and worked for the NAACP Legal Defense and Educational Fund. In 1967, Marian met and fell in love with Peter Edelman, a Harvard law school graduate, while he was an assistant for then U.S. attorney general Robert Kennedy. They married in 1968—1968! They are still married and have successfully raised three children, all boys. How could a black woman, who worked for the NAACP, Martin Luther King Jr., and the SCLC and fought for the equality and justice for black people marry a white, Jewish man? Simple. They shared values.

Sophia A. Nelson, forty-two, also an attorney, advocates for issues impacting African American women, and the author of *Black Woman Defined,* is dismayed that black women are often so boxed in because for so many of us, the intertwined political and racial issues about whom you date are some kind of outward expression of your loyalty (or disloyalty) to the race—a conundrum black men who do the same don't seem to have. "Why can't I love a person who doesn't share my skin color and still advocated for my race?" asks Sophia. "I have wrestled with feeling this, because I've dated white men in high school and college and still am very much a proponent of 'black love.' I struggled with the fact that I have been in a relationship with a white man whom I adore. I hope we get married. It has nothing do with his whiteness, but I love his character, I like myself when I'm with him. You fall in love with a person regardless of their color. I think black women have to give themselves permission to love the people who will give them love. Every sister for herself now."

Clearance #3: *It's okay to want someone on the same income and education level as you, and it doesn't make you a gold-digger.*

If you are educated and upwardly mobile in your career, you should not have to apologize for wanting someone who is at, near, or exceeds your income level. Maybe you traveled abroad when you were in college, and a whole new world opened to you. Perhaps the illuminating philosophies you were exposed to in college makes you long to share your wisdom with a partner. But since 1.4 million black women go to college compared to 900,000 of black men, you might notice that the higher up you go in your education and career, the less black men there will be at the top of the rung to meet you.

"To start, they might find themselves in better relationships. Some professional black women would no doubt discover that they are more compatible with a white, Asian or Latino co-worker or college classmate than with the black guy they grew up with, who now works at the auto shop," says Ralph Richard Banks.

Clearance #4: *It's okay to have a preference—either way.*

I should say upfront that if you have a preference to only date within your race, *it's okay.* Janice and I did not write this book to in-doctrinate, cajole, or frighten you into doing something you have no desire to do. I will offer one piece of advice, however: *Don't wait or pray for God to bring you a husband while you play no active part in finding your ideal black man.* If you are a professional black woman looking for a professional black man, I strongly recommend you invest in a matchmaking service or join organizations in which you can meet unattached black men that meet your standards as a mate.

Conversely, if you are a black woman who has always had a fondness for nonblack men, congratulations—there's a lot in this book that will be helpful to you. More important, preferring someone not of the same race does not make you some self-hating freak. Many of the readers of my blog have never dated within their race—both male and female. When I probe about why they have this preference, it often stems from some grade school crush or a kind, older person who left an indelible impression upon them.

One commenter who goes by the screen name Nikki, said, "My first crush was a cute little blond, blue-eyed boy in kindergarten! I have preferred them ever since! But that does not mean I don't love [my] dad, uncles, cousins, close friends or drool over (umm . . . hello, Common, Boris Kodjoe, Idris Elba, yummy!) black men. But as far as sexual attraction, my preference is a tall, skinny, blond, blue-eyed man. I have no self-hatred, issues . . . it is just what I like."

Be glad you live in a time where you are (more or less) free to outwardly express your preference for swirling. After hearing Brenda's story, I don't know how anyone was brave enough to do it before the groundbreaking, *Loving vs. The State of Virginia.*

Brenda met her first love when she was twelve. And the object of her affection, Butch, was thirteen. During those innocent first days, they teased and frolicked under the lazy Georgia sky, gazing into each other's eyes, holding hands, and smiling. Butch's father, the wealthy man that he was, made light of it. "I was part of a community who came to work on his large farm. [The crush] was okay. He thought it was cute." After the harvest, years passed without them seeing one another, but they exchanged occasional phone conversations—nothing too heavy, just shooting the breeze. But then they came of age—that time when one touch and a certain look can spark something that often couldn't be stopped. Passion grew from anticipation—that gap of time between their next encounter, perhaps when they finished the day at their separate, segregated schools. After all, it was the 1960s. Brenda was sixteen and Butch was seventeen. She was black, he was white. A scandalous mix for that time, yet they dared. "It was the first time I ever felt love stirring in me. When I looked into that boy's green eyes, I fell in love, and he loved me, too."

Brenda, now in her sixties, has never had a preference for any other race except Caucasian, even when it was hard, even when it didn't work out, even when it could have gotten her killed. "I used to wonder why God would give me this preference, but I know in my heart it's because he knew I could handle it—even in south Georgia in the 1960s."

Just as some black women prefer non-black men, many non-black men have prefer black women. Charlie, age fifty-five and white, went on his first date with a black girl in 1974 when they were both seniors in high school. "At the time, it was a dangerous thing to do. For both of us!" he recalls. He's always admired the physical traits typical of black women—smooth, dark skin, lips, and teeth—but he always admires their character. "All the black women I've been with were intensely loyal and made me feel as if I was the most important thing in their lives. That combination is a great feeling to luxuriate in when you're a man."

Rich Fung, twenty-one, a gorgeous Filipino, Chinese, and Spanish hybrid, has always been drawn to African American women, too. "The thing I find attractive about black women is that black women are sure of themselves. They are self-aware, know what they have, and where they come from. This allows black women to constantly learn and grow and improve, becoming a better person through every decision they make.

"A lot of black women know what they want, or where they want to be in life, and I find that incredibly admirable. Their mind-set is not that of a pretty girl, but a beautiful woman."

Scott Barry Kaufman, PhD, thirty-one and a nonpracticing Jew, is an evolutionary psychologist who jokes that he should conduct a study on himself (personality and mating practices are his specialties) because he has always had an attraction to black women and their curvalicious bodies.

There are literally millions of men all over the planet who desire you, so if you're ready to expand your fishing from the pond to the ocean, get ready, because you'll be casting a mighty wide net.

NOTE: *None of the above is any attempt at brainwashing black women into dating interracially. If you prefer black men, great; but you should probably stop reading.*

CHAPTER FIVE

Christelyn

Is It Time to Edit the List?

We all have the Mr. Dream Man list.

Before I met my husband and got married, my Mr. Dream Man list was short and sweet:

1. He must be taller than me because I am a shrimp and I did not wish my shortness on my yet-to-be-born male progeny.
2. He must be fine, fit, and have the requisite minimum penis size.
3. Brains were a plus, but not a deal-breaker.
4. He should probably be black because that's just more comfortable.
5. And, oh yeah, he must be fine.

No one in particular pushed me into assembling this list, it just happened through social osmosis, I guess. Plus, every other black girl, woman and her grandma implied or inferred that I should want that because to get it would mean, I WIN!

Win . . . what?

My list sucked eggs. It was superficial and vapid, and indicated just how clueless I was about what was important in a relationship.

Can I get extra points for having a short list, though? For some, the Mr. Dream Man List is longer than the Dead Sea Scrolls.

Take this one pretty thirtysomething who asked me to hook her up with a "quality" man, because she figured that among my 3,000-plus Facebook friends and 4,000-plus blog fans, I was bound to know somebody who fit the bill. She had a high-powered job and three children. Here's what she wanted:

- No matter the color, dude just had to be gorgeous. (She used Halle Berry's babydaddy, Gabriel Aubry, by way of example.)
- He had to have a high paying, high-powered job.
- Be an on-fire Christian and have an encyclopedic knowledge of Bible verses.
- Stand over six feet tall.
- Wear expensive clothes and shoes.
- Have the confidence of a male peacock.
- He had to love kids.
- . . . and puppies.
- . . . and rainbows.
- . . . and long walks on the beach and conversations mainly geared toward him telling her how fabulous she was.

Ms. Unicorn Hunter assured me that she doesn't just go for looks, and "the heart is what really matters." She just found that ugly guys just didn't have enough self-esteem for her taste.

Let's pause a moment for effect . . . okay.

The type of man this woman wants, in my experience, only exists in the land of pink mountains, vanilla skies, and glittery flowers. Even President Obama, who is the hottest ruler the free world has ever known, does not make the list, because he's never modeled for Gianni Versace or Calvin Klein.

Now I'm not here to join the pile-on from not-so-well-meaning critics that this young woman should *lower* her standards, but I'll be the first to say it might be high time to for her to *evaluate* them. How many of those requisites determine whether a man will respect and love, marry, and then stick around to help raise kids?

Take a quick look at your own personal checklist. If it is 99.9 percent composed of what you can see with only your eyes, you might need to sit back, have a cup of tea, and sip on that for a minute. Keep that list pliable. Make it do some yoga, so it (and you) can be flexible and open—your perfect man might be just outside those lines on the paper you're writing on.

What's Holding You Back . . . Really? The "Hotness" Trap

Bundles of studies have proven that with both sexes, physical attractiveness is at the top of the dating and mating rung. A guy friend of mine once told me that men, with every encounter with a woman, imagine what that woman would look like in missionary position.

Women might not be initially thinking about creative positions in the Kama Sutra to try on someone they first met, but looks definitely play a part. Perhaps women are a bit more forgiving if the man of interest is funny and smart, and displays a consistent ability to pay his bills on time. On the other hand some experts argue that as women make gains economically, looks are becoming more of a factor in determining how women pick, as we come less financially dependent on men. But unless your idea of a meaningful relationship comprises you looking at your own personal version of a Greek god, if looks are all he's got then get ready for a slow train wreck, and that's irrespective of whether or not you're independent, own a home, and can change a tire with one arm tied behind your back.

So what's the alternative? Date the progeny of Alien and Predator because he might make for a better boyfriend? No one is saying you should date and mate with a toad. But at the same time, no extra credit should be given to a man who treats you badly. Women put up with hot guys who treat them like trash every day. It blows my mind at what a girl will do for a fine man who could sell pants to a snake. Consider yourself warned: put up with all kinds of emotional ugly—like cheating or abuse, or the more benign but disconcerting and noncommittal partner just because you enjoy eating man-candy, at your own peril. Empty vessels are extremely hard to fill.

But don't beat yourself up too much; it's not unusual to pant for a hot-looking, confident guy. It's natural and serves its purpose from an evolutionary perspective, says Scott Barry Kaufman, an evolutionary psychologist and professor at New York University. The problem comes when girls mistake Super-

jerk for Super*man*. The man with all the "swagger" could just be a selfish, parasitical narcissist, because they tend to make very good initial impressions—they dress to impress, project confidence, lay on the charm, and say a bunch of clever stuff during conversation so we think they're witty. They seem perfect at first . . . but sometimes, what you *see* is *all* you get.

Do You have "Nelly" Syndrome?

Okay, I just made that syndrome up, but it works just the same to make my point. Nelly, with his caramel skin, tight muscular body, brilliant smile, and full lips, with that naughty-boy twinkle in his eyes, is delish. And despite the fact that he ran a credit card down the crack of a woman's ass (and is pretty clear through his music and personal life that he most enjoys woman for hedonistic purposes), if I were single and we were trapped in a room at the Ritz Carlton he'd only have to chase me around the bed a couple times before it would get very hot in there, and I'm pretty sure clothes would be shed. Nelly is like sweet potato pie or cheesecake with whipping cream drizzled with chocolate— oh so good and oh so, so bad. Now that we've established my visceral lust for this man, let's talk about the not-so-sexy stuff, like when my oldest daughter, at only four-year-old, was singing, "It's gettin' hot in herre, so take off all ya cwoos!" That made me pause, because fast-forward twenty years and picturing her being chased by her Nelly contemporary gave me goose flesh. I didn't want the bad boy or his like anywhere near my baby. So why would I want him for myself?

"Women go for bad boys because they don't feel as though they deserve a good guy and women fear the intimacy that good guys offer. Also, bad boys are more of a challenge, sexually exciting and forbidden," says Carol Lieberman, a psychiatrist and author of *Bad Girls: Why Men Love Them & How Good Girls Can Learn Their Secrets.*

If you're (un)lucky enough to hook up with a bad boy, don't think you've won a prize. Evia Moore, who's credited as the pioneer advocate of black women dating interracially through her blog *Black Female Interracial Marriage Ezine,* coined the term "DBR," an acronym for "Damaged Beyond Repair." DBR's can be any color or gender, young or old. These are the people you can't fix no matter how much your try, and worse, trying to "fix" often leads you to becoming broken. Bad boys are often DBRs, and whether they function well in their career or can't keep a regular job, they're ability to trust and bond is crippled by things in their past that are beyond your ability to love it away, chica.

Are IBMs Your Problem? (And No, We're Not Talking About the Corporation)

The big inkblot on your list might be your desire for an IBM—The Ideal Black Man. Individual preferences may vary, but usually, the "IBM" is more than six feet tall, devilishly handsome, optimally went to an Ivy League school, and makes a kajillion dollars a year. He loves his mama, who raised him alone and sent him to college with all the quarters she saved from the moment he was born. Sound about right? I'll admit it—he does sound good. And if you're an IBW, you surely deserve an IBM. After all, every great man should want an equally great counterpart, right? But what's wrong with an Ideal Mexican Man, an Ideal Japanese Man, or an Ideal Puerto Rican Man?

Some people think race is a deal breaker—it's black or nothing. But what about a man who enjoys traveling, or likes to go to the movies, or travel? I'd hate to see women miss out on someone special because they're holding out for a man who meets the checklist. This is more and more true as the pendulum swings from very successful and educated blacks and those who may be mired in an underclass culture whose experience is wholly separate from the latter group. Black people are more different than they've ever been. Black people are varied—we have black men in the White House and black men who don't even know where the White House is. You have lots of people who are cut off, they don't know people who go to college or go to work every day, and the only thing you have in common is skin color. It doesn't make much sense to limit yourself. "You might find the qualities you want in someone from Spain, Libya, or Idaho," says Ralph Richard Banks, who himself might be what you'd call an IBM—he graduated from Harvard, never went to jail, has no stray babies, and has been married for fourteen years. But that's the problem—he's taken.

Where are all the legitimately "good" black men, who are educated, gainfully employed, handsome, funny, tall, and chocolate? They're out living life or so it seems. Like you should be. Educated and financially stable black men have their pick and consider themselves free agents, coveted by women across the melanin spectrum. Alena, a New York University graduate student in her late twenties, summed up her experience, which unfortunately is not unique.

> *I've met what my friends call IBMs who meet the financial and educational requirement part of the list but they have not been interested in monogamy, seem disinterested in marriage and family, and have hyperinflated egos. I've been told on numerous occasions by men of this ilk that they don't have to focus on settling down right now as they are hot stocks—"I have a degree, I go to work every day, I've never been to jail, and I don't have more than one babymama" . . . I don't feel like I should have to give a brother $200 for passing Go! Like, I'm supposed to lower my standards because you did what you are supposed to do? Congrats on avoiding the prison industrial complex, but that doesn't give you a pass to ride this ride. Another guy told me that he doesn't even have to buy his own underwear or wash his own clothes because different women do it for him.*

One online commenter gave a pretty raw comment on a story published in *Madame Noire*, an online publication catering to upwardly mobile black women, called, "This is Why You're Single . . . Fellas Edition." The list was fair game, since there's been a boatload of magazine articles, television specials, and books trying to decipher the single-black-woman enigma. So what's good for the goose is apparently not good for one online blogger with a trollish name, who had some choice words to the author of the piece:

lmao I didn't view the list, don't need to. None of the reasons on it will ever keep a woman from fu*king us or if it would we wouldn't let them find out until after we got them in the bed. So as long as men are getting sex we can care less if we're in a relationship or not or if we're single. Being single is better than being in a relationship anyway because it's a lot easier having sex with multiple women without any of them snooping through cells, questioning where you been and who with, constantly nagging or accusing you of cheating and you save more money she would expect you to spend on dates, gifts for her, and other nonsense. You can tell them you're seeing other women and they can't do sh!t about it but leave and if they do, who cares because you still have another chick to call on for those needs we like women to fulfill, so she lost that competition. Silly women, always thinking men are the same or want the same things as FEMALES. =)

A guy with a crude name was quick to add:

but he is telling the truth.... 90% of men wish they could be that man that you just described.... no man wants to be the good guy that you want a relationship with... then we would have to be around you all the time... and have to listen to you bump your gums all the time.... feed us and fuck us and shut the fuck up until it's time to feed us and fuck us again.... that is pure bliss ... if we want conversation... we will start one up... until then ... leave us the hell alone and take your problem to that squareycube guy who just listens to you ramble all day about us...

Well, alrighty then. These disgusting comments are extreme, but there's a bit of truth at the core: If men feel like getting a woman is as simple as waiting at the station for the next freak train—which comes every hour except on Sundays—then what incentive would a man have to settle in and play house? And if he's an IBM, the chances get slimmer and slimmer as that man's wallet gets fatter and fatter, says Banks.

Here's the snag: 44.8 percent of black women graduate from U.S. colleges and universities, compared to 33.1 percent of their black male counterparts. More black women hold powerful, high-paying corporate jobs while black men are lagging in this area. This trend has led to some cultural shifts that don't bode so well for black girls, because black boys navigate toward the allure of having swag and quick and easy money, while black girls are encouraged to go to college because they can't (or shouldn't) expect a man to take care of them. We're discouraged to date outside our race, and then told to "lower our standards" and that "our degrees won't keep us warm at night." So what choice do we have?

We don't have many if we don't explore all our dating options, and the lopsided achievement status can cause major relationship woes. Carolyn Edgar, a divorced mother of two, Harvard graduate, and practicing attorney, bent herself into a pretzel to make "black love" work for her. She was the professional with a lower-achieving husband. "I went to a Christie's auction, bought myself a three-carat diamond and platinum Harry Winston engagement ring, and planned a small wedding. At our divorce trial, my ex told the judge I 'forced' him to get married," she said.

She was the high wage earner, which, he said, made him feel "less than a man."

I asked her why she limited herself to only dating black men, and she couldn't exactly put her finger on it, but told me she had a "what about the children?" attitude about it. She also had an aunt who married a white man during the 1960s and remembers that all the talk throughout the family was about how hard so-and-so had it, how Aunt What's-her-name wasn't accepted by Uncle What's-his-name's family. And by the way, Auntie and Uncle What's-Their-Name are still happily married.

In retrospect, she thinks back to the nonblack men who were interested in her in law school, and has some regrets about how quickly she dismissed the possibility of a relationship with them. "All that self-imposed limiting is crap you do to yourself," she says. Perhaps what is even more ironic is that the one student who she was interested in told her, "I like you, but I could never take you home." He was black. He also came from a wealthy, well-connected family that approved of his white British girlfriend (who apparently was from aristocracy) over Carolyn from Detroit.

So Carolyn was not only gun-shy to marry interracially, but also faced insecurities about class. So she went back to what she knew, because as an attorney, she felt the need to prove she didn't think she was better than anyone else since she became a fancy-schmancy lawyer. Some advice she would give to her younger self? "Get out and enjoy and explore your options, and don't attach yourself to one person. Date people who think differently than you do. If you stick with what you know you end up stuck."

CHAPTER SIX

Christelyn

How to Go from Mr. Rainbeau to Mr. Right

First let's understand the double standard.

The first time my extended family saw my husband was at my uncle's funeral. First, second, and third cousins flew out from Texas to pay their respects to my father's much loved brother, who died at eight-three from emphysema. Before the funeral, in the living room of my late uncle's San Francisco town house, I passed pictures of my husband and baby daughter around the room, beaming. Frankly, I was proud. I was one of the youngest people there who was married. And to their child's father even. Yet, what I got was a lot of muffled snickers and people tripping over their words. They looked at my husband like he was from Uranus. It was annoying, especially since I knew of several black male cousins who had dated and mated with white women, and I saw the byproducts of such unions running around the family property. There are more than twenty biracial children in my family, mainly the result of black men with white, Asian, or Hispanic women. These unions were universally accepted by both male and female cousins, and not much was said about the nonblack mothers of the kids, aside from a few remarks about how the white mothers didn't do their children's hair as neatly as they would have liked.

But as for me? I felt like a circus side act. The double standard and hypocrisy of it all just pissed me off. I didn't say anything at the time, but I felt a mixture of embarrassment, rejection, and indignation. How could these same relatives, my own blood, laugh or just remain speechless at my wonderful, beautiful husband, who made me so spectacularly happy and was such a loving father to a child not his own and our newly born little bubble of love, Chloe? I couldn't figure out what was funny to them. My husband is very handsome with a million-dollar smile, so . . . it couldn't be his looks. It was because he was white or perhaps nonblack. I guess to them, a white guy married to and loving a black woman was inappropriate, but it was perfectly acceptable for my black male cousins to procreate with a white, Asian, or Latina woman.

Why was it okay for the black guys, and not the black girl? Wasn't I entitled to find love and happiness, too, even if it wasn't with a black man? My fiftyish cousin Wanda, among the gathering of speechless family members, later explained to me what was going on in her head. She basically said that seeing a black woman with a white man was something so completely unusual to her, while seeing her black nephews intermixing was as natural as humidity and mosquitoes in Texas in July. But a white man with a black woman? It was cause for suspicion. She was worried about whether my husband would try to exploit me in some way. That was never a concern the other way around, however.

As a child of the 1980s, I witnessed the gradual acceptance of black men dating outside their race. But it hadn't happened without a fight. *Waiting to Exhale*, with a dash of *Jungle Fever*, anyone? Black women felt hurt, angry, and rejected, and they weren't shy about expressing themselves. After all—things were getting good.

Whether explicitly and implicitly, to some degree black women have accepted the idea that they should fall back and let black men enjoy their newfound privileges. It was like being a black Rosie the Riveter, except we didn't have comfortable homes and a housewife's lifestyle to return to. Even cornerstones of black media, like *Ebony* and *Essence*, joined in the propaganda. *Essence* ran a piece in 1970 telling newlywed black women to discard their independence and "make [their husbands] feel 10 feet tall." A decade later, a disillusioned editorial lamented, "Many women who followed this philosophy ended up worn-out, broke, and confused when their husbands got bored and left them for white women."

So here we are, a half century later, and most black women are still sacrificing their own health and happiness to keep black love/hope alive, and black men are (and have been doing what they've wanted) for ages, dating and marring whomever they wish. In some circles, it's almost expected that wealthy, accomplished black male athletes or the highly educated and upwardly mobile black men will marry a nonblack woman. Carolyn Edgar, the Harvard Law School graduate we highlighted in chapter 5 was told by another a male black student, who came from an accomplished black family, that he could never take Carolyn home. After all, she was from Detroit. His parents much more approved of his white British girlfriend, who was allowed into his family home with open, eager arms.

So why the white girls? "One possibility is the (sometimes unconscious) idealization of 'whiteness,'" says Dr. Mikhail Lyubansky, a professor and lecturer of The Psychology of Race and Ethnicity at the University of Illinois. "For black men, a white woman may represent the forbidden fruit. To have a white girlfriend/wife is to have what white America explicitly forbade until the 1960s, and even today seems to resent. Apart from the usual qualities that men might find attractive, for men of color, a white woman also may have the extra appeal of having something they were told they couldn't have: a door into the privileges of white society."

Black men can be problack and mate and marry white women (e.g., Harry Belafonte, Quincy Jones, Sidney Poitier, Huey Newton), but black women shall not do any such thing without getting the gigantic, hairy eyeball.

And what of the double standard in this? At some point, black women gave up fighting against their men coupling up with nonblack women. But like my cousins who giggled at the face of my white husband, the black community has yet to universally accept black women pursuing their own happiness with nonblack men. We are downright discouraged to do so. We're told that, "No white man would ever want us, or no rainbeau can love us like another black man, that the only reason anyone of another color would ever want a black woman is because of some freaky fetish. Who's telling black women these things? Our mother, sisters, brothers, friends, and perfect strangers you meet at Walmart.

Kola Boof, womanist and author of *The Sexy Part of the Bible*, sees the disparity between the freedom black men have when choosing a mate versus the slim pickings black women have. "Even my nonblack editors—Jewish, Indian, Hispanic—see it. They tell me they go to the club and all the black girls are standing around with no one to dance with while the black men seem to ignore them. The only time a black man pays a black woman any attention is when he sees her dancing with a white man," says Boof, who is of Sudanese decent.

As an African, I deeply believe in black men being with black women. That is my base desire. But I'm talking about what the facts of our society are. In America, it is not set up where that is possible, and it's even worse in the U.K. Now if I were a mother, I would have to be for my daughters, and tell my daughters the truth. [Black women] need to forget about this whole "loyalty" thing because they have none for you. And if there is no loyalty, then you are a fool to stand around pining for a phantom. We only have one life as we know, so you might as well go out there and live your life and love your blackness within your own space. Because we cannot force black men to affirm us.

We cannot force them to love Africa and want to see black children. I talk to millions of black women. I know black women love black children. I know that we want black men. There's not a thing like that, where millions of black women don't want black men. In our videos, we love to see Blair Underwood. We love a dark-skinned, shirtless black man. But we don't have a choice anymore, sisters. We are being pushed into such a space that all we can do is stand for what we stand for personally and individually. There is no real black community.

Now I don't present all this stuff to depress the hell out of you, or make rainbeau dating some kind of pissing match to see which gender can outdo the other with interracial dating. Kola's right. Most black women do want to be with black men—and that included me at one time in my life. I wanted someone like my dad: a 100 percent dedicated, ride-or-die family guy, good sense of humor, a love of children and puppies, smart, good with money, and a super Mr. Fixit. As it turns out the man who was just like my father was a WASP: yep, a White Anglo-Saxon Protestant from Westport, Connecticut.

What Does the Ideal Rainbeau Look Like?

When you think of the type of man who, like you, is open to exploring interracial and intercultural relationships, does a picture of him come to mind? I remember back in high school there was the "token" white boy who was adopted and accepted into the cool black-boy clique because he had somehow convinced the crew that his whiteness was some cruel cosmic mistake, and he should have been born a brother. He had adopted the swagger, the slang, the affinity for rap and R&B, and wore his hair in a fade. And of course, he loved the sisters. And because this guy was so black-culture identified, it was therefore acceptable to date him, because after all, it wasn't *his* fault that he was a black panther trapped in a polar bear's body.

And while you might think only the type of guy from the movie, *Zebrahead* (the Detroit version of *Romeo & Juliet*) might be interested, I'm here to tell you how 1,000 percent wrong you are. But in a nice way, of course.

Bottom line: It doesn't matter what kind of clothes he wears, what music he listens to, how he votes, how many black women he's dated, or how many black friends he has, the ideal rainbeau dater does not look or act any way in particular, so it's not likely you'll be able to spot him in a crowd surrounded by a cluster of other black dudes who are laughing at his jokes and smacking him on the back. And even then, there's no guarantee that he'll have the qualities you want in a man. So stop looking for superficial cues, because the answer to what an ideal rainbeau looks like starts in the mind.

> **The ideal rainbeau dater does not look or act any way in particular, so it's not likely you'll be able to spot him in a crowd.**

Throughout my hundreds of interviews and interactions with black women who have happily mated or married interracially, four common characteristics always seemed to be attributed to the man, no matter what race, religion, or culture: rainbeaus are critical thinkers, they've forged their own life paths without apologies, were not easily influenced by peer or familial pressure, and had oodles of integrity.

INDEPENDENCE/CRITICAL THINKER

The ideal guy is independent in all things—career, philosophy, and most often, politics. He is a critical thinker, and has his own mind. He processes the world through his own ideological prism. He weighs the benefits and risks of his relationships by staying true to his own happiness and fulfillment.

Take my husband, a straight-laced New Englander who votes republican. He has no idea who Eric B and Rakim are and thinks Tyler Perry movies are stupid. His favorite store is J.Crew and he did cotillion as a child. But besides dancing a very good waltz, he is rhythm challenged. In other words he's a whitey-white boy who before he met me had never dated a black woman. "I think that in a way, in how we met [in a Yahoo chat room], it wasn't about what color you were. We laughed and had a good conversation, and that's what attracted me first. The fact that you were cute was a plus," says Mike Karazin—my better half.

Things were easy for a while when it was just us. But when we started to get serious and he told his parents about me, they were less than thrilled. His mother was concerned about the weirdness of it all. She never in her life had a black friend. On the other hand, when she lived in the South for a short time after marrying my father-in-law she went to a Laundromat that hung a sign that read "Whites Only." She was confused about this, and asked another person where the heck she was going to wash her colored clothes if this was a facility for only white clothes. The woman looked at her, bewildered. "Lady, 'Whites Only' means no black folks allowed in here." Essentially, she had no experience with Jim Crow, and never had to think about black people at all—she never intersected with them in her social network. This idea of having a black daughter-in-law scared the bejeezus out of her. My father-in-law, who was a judge in criminal and family court, advised Mike against legitimizing our relationship for two reasons: As a family court judge, he reflected that people who were more alike and who came from similar race and socioeconomic backgrounds had a better chance of staying married. Second, he flat-out thought our union would be bad for my husband's career prospects.

I'm going to pause the story here, because the apprehension Mike's parents had was our tipping point, our fork in the road. Mike was faced with making a key decision that either way would affect the rest of his life: bend under the pressure of his parent's disapproval and dump me, or make a calculated decision based on what he wanted for his life. Unlike a romantic "love will conquer all" attitude complete with horse blinders, you want your guy to know exactly what he's in for when he forges a relationship with you. He has weighed the positives and potential negatives, and comes out firmly knowing what he wants: you.

"I came to the point where despite the differences in how we looked, I wanted to be with someone I really loved, and you were that person. You want your parents to approve of who you're with, but at the end of the day you have to live your own life."

Less than a month later, Mike presented me with not one but *two* engagement rings.

GOOD RAINBEAUS BEAT TO THEIR OWN CONGA: A LONER: A LEADER

Forget the cliché that the only rainbeaus down to date a black girl are wanna-bes and über-liberals with something to prove to the world. Most of the men who are married to the thousands of readers on my blog are just regular, middle-of-the-road in their politics with absolutely no desire to be the next Vanilla Ice.

Coupled with an independent mind, the ideal man to forge a lasting relationship is often an oddball. And by "oddball" I don't mean "crazy." He probably wasn't the most popular guy in high school, and he didn't care. He was probably the smartest or most creative. He's the guy that might not have pledged for a fraternity in college because he thought they were a bunch of dweebs and drunks. He is almost never the "see and be seen" type. If he wears designer clothes he does so because they look good and last longer than anything he would buy at Walmart.

One of my favorite commenters, Penny, on Beyond Black & White summed up the ideal rainbeau so well I could not have said it better myself. So I won't and just let her tell you:

> There was an archetype male character that was popular for decades in American literature and movies and that was the loner/leader. He didn't have a lot of friends (if any) and he lived by his own strong moral code. Think of Humphrey Bogart's character in Casablanca, *Gregory Peck's character in* To Kill a Mockingbird, *Steve McQueen's character in* Bullitt, *Kevin Costner's character*

in The Untouchables, *etc. Men who didn't care what others thought, men that didn't suffer fools or cowards, men who did what they wanted to do instead of what other people wanted them to do, but they could always be counted on to do the right thing. It seems to me that a lot of the nonblack men who date and have successful marriages to black women share a lot of the attributes of those loner/leader characters. You have to have a certain amount of resolve and inner toughness, you have to have a strong personal compass and you have to be able to brush off obstacles other people try to put in your way.*

The Loner/Leader is often his own boss or is in a high-powered position. He lets his work speak for itself. He's often in his position because of his outlook on life—secure in himself, free thinking, open-minded, and beholden to no one's approval.

HIS POLITICS

A sample survey I conducted of 157 *Beyond Black & White* readers revealed some surprising results about the philosophies and political views of men who were happily matched with black women. Nearly 40 percent of the voters said their guys were moderate and not beholden to any particular political party. Twenty-eight percent leaned toward conservative politics, and only 17 percent of the female respondents said their partners were flaming liberals raised by hippies.

Of course, there are extremes. Surprisingly—and this floored me, 17 percent of respondents said their rainbeaus were card-carrying NRA members who worship at the church of Ronald Reagan.

The most notable example I know is the gun-loving, Fox-news watching lover of black women, Craig Radala, forty-seven, of Michigan. Craig, a corrections officer, loves NASCAR, is a libertarian, thinks the NAACP has become a racist organization and . . . thinks black women are the most beautiful in the world. He's divorced and has two biracial children, a boy and a girl.

The wife of such a white-bread respondent said this:

Hubby is the offspring of suburban-living, yacht-club-membered, card-carrying Republicans. He grew up in a privileged and closed world. To them Ronald Reagan was God and people of color were there to serve. Because of his education and the work he did Hubby traveled extensively across country and the world and came in contact with different types and kinds of people. This changed some of his perspectives markedly. He is still conservative when it comes to money and finance. He makes no apology for his (now our) wealth and privilege. He believes in hard work and sees nothing wrong with the haves having and the have nots not having. He does not believe in the government mandating the transfer of wealth to others. That should be done privately since the haves owe a duty to the have nots.

And sometimes the tree-hugging liberal whose heart bleeds for the downtrodden doesn't just date black girls as a political statement. "My beau is a tried-and-true liberal Dem. While most people will caution you about dating über-liberal guys, sometimes they are using you to prove their political convictions and out of white middle class guilt, my country club born and raised

WASP is authentic in his intentions both toward me and politically," says another respondent. Another one said her man was a straight Commie. "He's a member of the Socialist party. Yes really," said one respondent to the survey.

Caution: Having an independent-mind does not equate to "rebel." By definition, a rebel is a person who resists authority, control, or convention. Jails are chock-full of rebels. Rebels get in trouble. They can't keep a job. They have an almost desperate need to buck the system (think that guy at the bar who's always spoiling for a fight before he's even finished his first beer). And rebels are mostly big babies who want you to burp them and change their diapers and crash on your couch.

AT WORK: AVOID THE NINETY-POUND WEAKLING

Let's talk a bit about what the guy you shouldn't be dating might look like. I caution women who contemplate relationships with a man who obsesses or frets about what everybody thinks of him. In his work life, he lives and dies upon the approval of what his coworkers and superiors think of him, not only professionally, but personally. My advice? Stay away from these eager-to-please beavers, because if there is even a whiff of disapproval about him dating you, he'll either hide you in the closet or dump you like a trash truck.

There's nothing wrong with wanting an ambitious man. In fact, I encourage it. BB&W reader, Chrissy, twenty-six, says her man, thirty-four, is a go-getter but is proud to have her by his side. "I am a lawyer dating a soon-to-be lawyer who is white. My experience in the legal profession is that the majority of [lawyers] are ladder-climbers in one way or another. I am more of a 'carve out your own niche' type lawyer, but my boyfriend is a total corporate, big firm, intense, 'keep on the lookout for something that gives you an edge and is always on the move' type. Although he is a total ladder-climber and would do what it takes to be successful in his firm, it has nothing to do with our relationship and he has only wanted to show me off instead of hide me in a closet."

But give up on a man who is willing to cave because some coworker says, "Nice black chick you got there, but what will Mr. Big think? Don't you have a promotion coming up?" Let the little wuss cuddle up to his promotion at night and leave him the heck alone.

STAY AWAY FROM "THE MAMA'S BOY" OR THE "DADDY PLEASER"

Parental influence, especially pressure put on by a mother, is a formidable force that might not be worth the fight in the long run. A man completely beholden to his parents' approval will always crave it. That means you come second until the day they die. I have an old college friend who once dated a forty-year-old Danish man whose mother had access to his e-mail account and called him three to four times a day. And surprise! She didn't approve of his choice in girlfriends and explicitly said she would not approve of any marital union between him and my Caribbean acquaintance. We lost touch, but I'd give a good guess that the outcome. . . .

Then there's the guy who wants Daddy to approve of everything he does because to let daddy down is to disgrace the family name. Dad is the alpha in the father/son relationship and sternly dictates his son's education, career, and marriage prospects. He's the dad who might say, "You can sleep with a black woman, but don't you bring one home!"

Fielding "Mr. Right"

Now that you know what a serious swirler acts like, it's your job to filter the trolls from the princes, the wheat from the chaff. But you can't go on your first date with a list of questions about your date's political affiliations, relationship with his parents, or whether or not he's the company kiss-up. Too many personal questions on the first date is a no-no, and those kinds of questions are borderline Gestapo.

Go by the three-date-rule. First date is about compatibility and attraction, second date is more of the same, third date lets you know if you really want a fourth or fifth one. During the course of dates one through three, you can pick up on certain behaviors that may indicate whether or not Mr. Rainbeau will turn out to be Mr. Right.

The Three-Date Checklist

Location, location, location:

Where is Mr. Potential taking you for your first date? If it's in his apartment because he wants to cook you dinner, that's a red flag. For your own safety a first date should be in a public place. And if a guy only wants to meet you in secret, chances are he doesn't want to be seen in public with you. Lastly, "cook you dinner" is often code for "Come over for wine and frozen pizza on my turf so I can seduce you out of your panties."

Shifty Eyes: Take note of a man who isn't focusing on you, but on whether or not people are looking at the two of you. This guy cares way too much about what people think and is *not* his own man.

Sex Talk Too Early: This goes for *any* guy. If your date gives suggestive sexual talk anytime on the first date, run. This guy's not interested in you as a whole [hole, haha!] person—just the reproductive parts.

He Acts Like He Doesn't Know You in Public: The only time a guy should walk ahead of you in the Western world is to open the door for you. He doesn't have to be mushy and display lots of PDA, but he should make it clear that he is out *with you*.

He Has a Preoccupation with Your Blackness: Of course you want your date to think you're hot. He may comment on the lovely tone of your skin, the cotton-softness of your 'fro, and how that dress you're wearing falls and clings in all the right places. But if he starts with idiotic clichés, like "The blacker the berry, the sweeter the juice!" or "I just love eating chocolate!" it's time to exit, stage left.

Find Out If He Lives at Home with His Parents . . . Pronto: Yes, it's a slow economy, and living with your parents for a brief stint isn't unusual these days. But when a guy lives with his parents, it's their house and their rules. As a side note, it is not unusual for an Asian or Italian man to live at home with his parents until he gets married. But again, the parental influence is strong, and if Mommy and Daddy don't approve, chances are you'll be the one getting the boot.

Observe How He Treats Other People: Observe, observe, observe. Dating is about gathering data, so best to get as much as you can before you get attached. Does he speak to the waiter or waitress respectfully or with disdain? Is the whole date about how he hates his mother, father, the French, or cuddly little puppies? Don't think you're special—he'll add you to the list if things don't work in his favor.

Let Him Talk: Eugenia Mitchell, author of the blog *Married Girl in a Weird World,* says that her experience working ten years as a paralegal helped her to home in her active-listening skills. "It was essential that I take in their words, dissect them, make conclusions," she said. We girls are so quick to fill in those awkward silences between the natural lulls in conversation, but sometimes it's best to fight the urge to chat incessantly about the weather. Casually ask open-ended questions that require more than a "yes" or "no" response, like "What did you like to do growing up?" (If his answer is that he likes to kill small animals and set cat's tails on fire, chances are he's a sociopath. Get where I'm going with this?)

Be Fluent in Body Language: Body language cues in three-date fielding are time and ovarian-saving essentials. Two sets of signals you should be attuned to are gestures that indicate lying or defensiveness. According to Allan and Barbara Pease, authors of the bestselling book *The Definitive Book of Body Language*, cues can almost never be controlled, because humans are mostly unaware they are doing them.

The difficulty with lying is that the subconscious mind acts automatically and independently of our verbal lie, so our body language gives us away.

COMMON INDICATORS OF DECEPTIVE COMMUNICATION

Mouth covering. Unless he's got a mouthful of food, covering the lips is often a giveaway that someone isn't being honest.

Rubbing the eyes. That's an easy one. He does it so he doesn't have to look at you when he tells that whopper.

Neck scratching. Look for constant and repetitive action.

Grabbing at the collar. It happens because the rise in body temperature and a man runs his finger around the rim of his collar to get some fresh air.

Ear grabbing. If you tell you date about how much you'd love to see the latest modern art exhibit at the museum and he replies with "Yeah; that sounds like fun," while pulling at his ear, chances are he'd rather have a root canal than see that exhibit.

Swiping at imaginary boogers (otherwise known as the nose swipe). Scientists over at the Smell & Taste Treatment and Research Foundation found that when you tell a fib, chemicals are released inside the nose, causing it to swell. But be careful with this one—make sure your date doesn't just have a cold.

What the Ideal Mate Looks Like

So what choice do we black women have, Mr. Thug Love or Corny Carlos? The ideal lies somewhere in the middle, says Dr. Kaufman. The bottom line, and the point of this book, is to choose *character* above *color*. Don't focus on "snagging a [fill in the race] man" just because you think that's the answer to all your problems, because jackassedness (I like this better than "asshole" ever since Obama called Kanye a jackass) comes in all shades.

THE ULTIMATE CHARACTER CHECKLIST

- Your ideal rainbeau man is independent-minded (not to be confused with reckless, rebellious, or just plain raunchy). *He thinks for himself.* This is also the most common and most distinctive characteristic of a man who dates, marries, and mates interracially.

- He takes pride in his work.

- He has a career direction and is gainfully employed. (Special exceptions are rainbeaus in law school, medical school, or business school.)

- He has integrity. He knows right from wrong and usually listens to the little angel on his shoulder. "Your long wish list of traits for your Mr. Wonderful should be negotiable, but [integrity and a moral compass] must be nonnegotiable. For example, if you find that man of integrity who thinks you are beautiful and would lay down his life for you, putting your needs above his own, you might want to cross 'dimples' off your list of requirements for your husband," says Kenneth Ryan, author of *Finding Your Prince in a Sea of Toads.*

PART II

---

*Put Yourself
Out There*

CHAPTER SEVEN

Janice

Why It's Worth It

Oh no! I could never marry a man who wasn't black—people would think I'd lost my mind!"

A friend of mine—let's call her Christine—is midthirties, tall, athletic, and shapely, with beautiful café au lait skin and a smile right out of a Rembrandt toothpaste ad. She has impeccable fashion sense—I've never seen her in the same outfit—or hair—twice. As outgoing as she is compassionate, she is a nurse who works with HIV/AIDS patients and often travels the globe on education and welfare missions, and in the past couple of years that I have known her, I've often heard the senior married gents in our neighborhood praying that Christine can find herself a "good black man," lest she become "yet another beautiful black sister languishing on the vine."

Twice, she tells me, she has turned down a marriage proposal from a professional football player in her hometown of Florida whom she has been dating covertly off and on for a number of years. Christine wants to be married and have children, but she fears her friends and family back home would think she had gone crazy for taking up with a white man. I'll admit I thought she was kinda nuts for letting that stop her. But then again, that way of thinking has never crossed my mind.

For as far back as I can remember, the kinds of men I was attracted to were never restricted to one race, culture, or even type. I had my posters of sandy-blond pop star Sean Cassidy and afro-wearing Michael Jackson side by side on my wall, eventually replaced by *The Dukes of Hazzard*'s John Schneider and *Miami Vice*'s Phillip Michael Thomas. They all looked good to me. (If I were to wallpaper my bedroom walls today, it would be a collage of Lenny Kravitz, Asian actor Karl Yune, Javier Bardem, Benicio Del Toro, and *The Mentalist*'s Simon Baker [okay, I guess I do have a thing for blond guys . . .]). My first crush was my physical education teacher in fifth grade: a man of slight but muscular build with (you guessed it) blond hair, blue eyes, and a beard—just like every picture of Jesus I'd ever seen. (Sure, I knew Jesus as Lord and Savior, but there was no denying the Son of God was a *hottie*.) And although growing up I lived in predominantly black neighborhoods and attended a predominantly black church, I had extended family members of other races; I went to school, and was friends with, all kinds of kids; and most of my closest childhood girlfriends, who are still my forever friends, are, with one exception, of mixed race. I had dated white guys in college (albeit much to my father's chagrin). I married a black man, whom my dad also didn't like, but he's pretty much an equal opportunity he's-not-good-enough-for-my-daughter kind of father.

After my divorce I continued dating all sorts of fellows of varying racial and cultural backgrounds. I relish in diversity, and refuse to be "colorblind," another construct of that "postracial" dream world. I don't have problems meeting men—just the rare ones who, like me, don't want to have children. In a lot of ways, this puts me in the minority of a minority, which makes dating out, for me, even more of a necessity—and, quite frankly, a lot more fun.

It is, of course, a little more complicated than that for many black women. It's complicated for most people, says David Knopes, PhD, a licensed clinical psychologist in Seattle, Washington, who specializes in behavioral and mental health. In his area of expertise, he deals with assessing the biological, psychological, and social factors that play into perceptions of our identity and how we choose to govern our lives. Basically, why we are the way we are.

Growing up as she did around mostly blacks in the South, with a less than favorable opinion of whites, certainly has had an impact on who Christine views as a suitable mate, as much as my upbringing has influenced mine. "Early lessons from childhood go into memory first, and what we were taught is always accepted as truth," says Knopes. "Everything that comes after that has to be assimilated or accommodated, which means it's folded into the rules you've learned or becomes a rule violation that makes the game more complicated," he says.

As Dr. Knopes points out, we're all social creatures, and as human beings, we most often rather follow a herd mentality than act like lone wolves. We all connect to things that are similar to us; the things that are different tend to make us to feel odd, unusual, or out of place. Of course, no one wants to feel like that. It's human nature to gravitate to what, and who, you know. But even that doesn't have to stop you from stepping outside your comfort zone. Despite the risks that may be inherent in dating out, and there are some, the benefits are so much greater.

Beyond his clinical expertise, Knopes, who is white, has been married for thirteen years to my friend and fellow scribe, Melanie McFarland, who is black. The two met back in the early nineties while students at Northwestern University in Illinois. At the time, she was a deejay at the university radio station, and he became captivated with the "funny, snarky, fast paced, hard-edge" personality he heard on the air, so refreshingly counter, he says, to the other "too-cool-for-school" jocks who hogged up the rest of the airwaves. "She was really powerful, and really fun," Knopes says. "She was like a celebrity to me." And when he finally got the chance to meet her—an introduction by his roommate who also had a crush on Mel, but never got up the nerve to ask her out—the woman behind the voice completely won him over, and the rest, as they say . . . well, you know what they say.

Their relationship has not been without the stares and whispers from passersby when they're holding hands; and the inaugural announcement of their dating to their parents sparked less than joyful first impressions. And yet, they are two of the happiest people. How did they manage it? For the answer, I decided to hop on the proverbial couch with Knopes, whom I, like Melanie, refer to as "Dave," to help me help you understand why this whole mixing thing scares us senseless, and why taking the chance is not only reasonable, but worthwhile. After a little over-the-phone catching up, we jumped right into it:

Me: *In my conversations with black women, I realize that the concept of dating out is not easy. But why is it still so difficult?*

Dave: I tell people that I work with as they're trying to sort out their identity, regardless of the issue, we all have three roads to take. Along those three roads we have a choice: The first, we upload the lessons from our childhood, usually our family or parents or whoever were the formative characters in our lives, and we can make their lessons our own, and we can proceed according to what we understood from what we were told. The second road is the opposite: We do everything the opposite of how we were told, a complete rejection: black is white, white is black, and that is very common in adolescence, just defiance for defiance's sake, but it can, for some people, be carried out into adulthood. The third option: We make our own road and we run a series of experimentations on what works for us and we hope it works out. That's usually a scarier road, but it's wrought with no more risks than the other two, and even possibly less.

The third road has been kind of what I have done in my own relationship with Mel: Proceed slowly, focus on the individual I was with much less than the concepts that were political, social, and racial. I dealt with those issues as they came up and [they] were barriers to people approaching us with their own projections of issues that we would now have to navigate that we didn't trigger outside our existence.

Me: *Dave, you make the third road sound so easy. But from what I've been hearing from black women, letting go of certain ideas about men of other races is pretty difficult.*

Dave: The third road is the scariest road. But it has the best chance of success because you're making decisions in the moment and you're paying attention to what you're doing, and hopefully getting to pick and choose from the successes and failed strategies of those who have gone before you.

Me: *Why is it so scary?*

Dave: It's the scariest because we're human. The first emotional response to all new things in any context is some form of fear until it is proven that it can be trustworthy and survivable. The way we are wired, that caveman part of our brains, is first avoidance before approaching. So in making our own rules and figuring out what works for us, we are confronted with that newness a lot more.

There's a study, and I wish I could attribute it, but I've never found it again after having read it once, but there were these two groups of skydivers, one were experts and the other were novices and they hooked them up to all kinds of biometrics: heart rate, respiration and skin responses. Then they pushed them all off a perfectly good aircraft. When they got on the ground, and they went through the data, and the biometrics of arousal in the body was identical for the experts as it was for the novices. Their bodies went through the same experience, but the experts—the people with experience who had learned to trust what was happening to them, who had ownership and a sense of control—

they talked about it as exciting, as exhilarating, a sense of being alive; of it adding fuel and spice to their lives.

The novices described it as terrifying, something to be avoided, as a ridiculous act. They talked about wanting to put the brakes on because it was new. They had no experience with that sensation and because it was they didn't trust it. We always mistrust what we don't know until we have more.

Me: *Considering your expertise on this subject goes beyond clinical, what are some of the areas couples need to begin thinking about when dating out?*

Dave: If we're going to take our own road, we'll be fighting, or assimilating and accommodating new information or new experiences, against what we were told the way it is—and that can be either true, or not true, depending on how all that went. Then the external forces, the social forces, that deals with the projection—and projection is anytime that I [am] doing something that distinguishes myself from the person who's looking at me; everything from the color of my hair, to the color of my skin, language, all of it. That person will be thinking about that, they will be aware of that violation, and the stuff that comes out of their mouths, should they choose to speak, will come out in the context where they *think* they're telling me about me: You shouldn't do this. That's not good. That looks bad. That's improper. That's only going to cause you heartache. But what that person is telling you is what's inside their own head. They're telling you what *they* would do. But they never package it that way because everyone thinks they're right.

Understanding that dynamic can make it easier to withstand some of the comments that come out that way, everything from well-intentioned and protective to simple and dumb-headed.

Me: *So just consider the source?*

Dave: Well, there's no protection from the rain. Just accepting our parents' values, or even rejecting them, runs the risk of catastrophic failure at the same rate as all the other choices have. So that conflict, every time you're seen with your partner who does not look like you, is butting into a lot of the same messages you've uploaded from your early development, and now you have a nice mix of old, internal information versus external information, and that could run the risk of seeming valid sometimes. But they're both just artifacts of how complicated it is to be human. Neither is true. Truth is defined by what works. Truth is defined by function.

Me: *If that's the case, then we should stop overthinking this thing and just do it.*

Dave: No, what I'm saying is open your mind, collect the information, and take good notes: Does this make you happy? Does this work?

And don't quit too early.

Work on fine-tuning the information, and understand where you come from and what people are projecting at you, and know there are a lot of moving parts in this game you're signing up for.

What I like about defining your own path is that it encourages people who do have their eyes open while they're doing these things to think about, consider, and understand more about the people they engage with. That brings a certain thoughtfulness to the relationship because you have to, on a regular basis, come up with the answer to the question: Why am I doing this?

And the reason why everyone goes through it—or the people who choose to go through it even put up with it, the additional headaches—is because it runs the risk of happiness, and at the end of the day happiness is the meaning of life.

Me: *"You run the risk of happiness"—that almost sound dangerous.*

Dave: Oh it scares the shit out of a lot of people.

And here's how it works: I call it Vietnam. In Vietnam, as long as we never stopped fighting we would never lose. But it was also impossible to live through. So if I start dating outside of my race, and it works out and it makes me happy, it invalidates all my previous strategies, all my previous thoughts, and I start to question: Why did I wait this long? What were my previous rules? That means that before this I was wrong? And that's something people avoid, confronting themselves with the idea that my life and my struggles up to this point weren't necessary; that we might not have been making the right sense out of the world. That's kind of a low-level crazy, and crazy is vulnerability. That weakness means you go from being in the herd to being some kind of prey. It is a high point of danger. That's why the delusional and the manic are generally not having fun. They're generally scared.

105

Me: *Fear seems to be a big part of this for African American women. Should they feel open enough with their partner to tell him, "This scares me"?*

Dave: If you don't discuss it with your partner (and in my experience with Mel, if it's not a conversation), then you end up living in one person's culture or the other. There isn't a blending, there isn't a coming together. Because in order not to make it weird, or not say "I do things differently where I come from," someone has to give, and in relationships we have to give on almost everything. There are only a couple of things that we can get really solid and firm, because it really is a game of flexibility, and it requires both you and your partner to have an individual identity. Otherwise, you just have a person with a shadow.

Me: *How do you begin that conversation when you have issues or concerns you want to address?*

Dave: You begin that discussion with "I" statements: *I* have been thinking about this . . . *I* saw this on TV . . . *I* talked with someone. You shouldn't tell people what *they* should be thinking about. Just explain the contents in your own head and see how your partner responds. This is not a projection; this is not a to-do list. This is an invitation and a disclosure: *I* have something on my mind . . . *I* was hoping you could talk to me about this . . . And it's usually done in stages; you don't just vomit the whole issues according to your current understanding. You start small and work your way into it.

Me: *Can you give me an example?*

Dave: Sure, one of the conversations that Mel and I would have in our early days in Chicago: We'd be out in Chicago and there would be a time when she would stop holding my hand and I wouldn't quite know what it was. Later, upon me asking about that behavior, it would be that she would be walking by other black men who were just giving her the stink eye and she was just not feeling the need to defend her decisions by way of these large numbers of oncoming strangers, and I remember telling her, "I didn't see anything," and her saying, "You don't look. These are not members of your culture. These are not people that you reference and usually expect eye contact and a smile or a nod from," when she was being good.

She was able to notice a definite deviation in behavior. Whereas me, I was quite used to the stink eye.

Me: *You were used to it?*

Dave: Yeah, when I'd come down to the Southside of Chicago to visit her in the early 1990s, many people were wondering what the hell I was doing. (laughs) But for the most part it was over-whelmingly just amusement on their part: Are you sure about that, man? May you walk with your God, son.

Thanks to Dave for the sage words of wisdom.

Okay, ladies, now let's get off the couch and get to steppin' out and find your rainbeau man!

CHAPTER EIGHT

Janice

You've Decided. Now Get Busy: 52 Ways to Find a Date

Don't know where to find that rainbeau guy? Dating out is as easy as simply getting out! It's possible to find a man anywhere. Perhaps a change of venue, or attitude, will make all the difference. Without trying, though, you'll never know.

As a happily single gal, I'm going to tell you something my blissfully married writing partner won't: Dating doesn't *have* to lead to getting hitched.

On the contrary, says Atlanta psychotherapist and relationship expert Joyce Morley, you date to have fun. (And a nice dinner wouldn't hurt.) "Most black women want to get with someone for a lifetime—they're looking for a husband, and they have this misbelief that they're supposed to be dating someone to be married.

"Black women will go out to dinner with a man and instead

of living in the here and now, they're living in the tomorrow," Morley says. "Just enjoy the guy! Find out more about him and *if* it gets to marriage, that's fine. Dating is all about having fun, but as black women, we haven't been given permission to have fun. Most black women are so heavy-laden and so serious about everything."

So, ladies, lighten up!

And, yes, while dating today can seem as competitive as finding a job, when looking for a man it's always best to begin from within: be yourself, be beautiful, be friendly, be open, and be positive. Your next boyfriend could be watching you before you even notice him. Start going down this list, and make your move. These are some of my personal out-of-your-box favorites. Granted, they aren't *fool*-proof (unfortunately, *those* are still out there). But with fifty-two weeks in the year, you could easily try one a week and find yourself off the couch and out on new adventures.

Dating is a journey, not the destination. So enjoy the ride. Your world is much bigger than you think!

1. Online Dating Is Still the In Thing. While this method of meeting prospective mates continues to carry a bit of a stigma, pretty much everyone does it at some point. I did. Beyond the well-known advertised hookup sites such as match.com, eHarmony.com, and interracialpeoplemeet.com, social media sites like Facebook, MySpace, Friendster, and even Twitter are becoming hot online spots for people to connect with others who have similar interests according to ehow.com. It's always best to be careful when meeting people online, especially if you have no mutual friends in common. So take necessary precautions, and don't be afraid to do an online background check if you feel the need. And remember, with this modus operandi, you're not aiming for *the one*. It's about having a good time, Leslie Oren suggests in *Fine, I'll Go Online! The Hollywood Publicist's Guide to Successful Internet Dating*. "I never say you're going to meet your husband online," Oren says about the book in an article I wrote for *emmy*®. "But the more you date, the more you date—just like getting traction with a celebrity, or a movie, or a television show." She cautions women from "pitching" someone other than themselves. Don't use dated photos or lie in your bio. If you want someone who is for real, let them see your genuine self.

2. Work It Out at Work. Various studies have noted that close to 80 percent of workers are either involved in, or knew someone who is involved in, a workplace romance. In fact, on-the-job romances are so common, research indicates that one-third of all relationships begin at work. (So for those of you still wondering where to find a mate, just peek over at the cute guy in the cubicle next to you and see if he's wearing a ring. If not . . . lunch date!) Consider women now comprise 45 percent of the U.S. workforce according to the Bureau of Labor Statistics, it creates an almost even playing field for hooking up with potential partners. That, and longer work hours are another factor—at least one in ten employees in the United States put in more than sixty hours per week on the job. Couple that with all this popular team-building business going on at companies and—presto!—a hot bed of intimate interaction is born between people who are apt to share the similar projects and job pressures, not to mention comparable educational and socioeconomic backgrounds. So, get a job where you can work with the public. Of course working from home makes it a lot harder to meet like-minded professionals—unless you move your "office" to a nearby Starbucks. If you're a writer, it's almost a no-brainer for a hookup.

3. Join a Church . . . Or Perhaps a New One. For those who believe that "a family that prays together, stays together," you're not alone. Studies have suggested that young adults, as well as a certain percentage of divorced or widowed folks, have met their spouses while at worship service or related church functions, and most reported a high level of satisfaction years after the wedding according to essortment.com. Some churches have subgroups allowing singles to mix and mingle—and even if you're not a member of a particular religious sect, these singles events and volunteer organizations within a particular house of worship can be excellent places to meet people. Not only will you be involved in something positive and potentially worthwhile, you'll also be expanding your personal network.

4. Everybody Needs a Vacation. Many more singles, and the tourism industry, are reaping the benefits of singles travel packages, where men and women can meet and share their *fantastic voyage*. (Cue the 1980s jam from Lakeside.) And with "voluntourism" (volunteerism through tourism) taking off, not only can you give back, but have a good time, too.

5. Get Your Hands a Little Dirty. Habitat for Humanity and Interracial Dating and Social Connections (IDSocialConnect), based in Washington, D.C., are great groups to join if you want to help put together homes for those less fortunate, while building something with someone new.

6. Head Back to School. In 2005, I enrolled at the University of Southern California's Masters of Professional Writing program where I not only expanded my writing horizons beyond journalism, but my dating pool. But you don't have to dive into a $40,000 private university education to meet men. According to essortment.com, taking a class, any class, will not only allow you to learn something new, but make new friends with similar interests, and starting a conversation is always easier when you have something in common.

7. Eat Out More. Busy, single men don't have time to cook, says stylecaster.com. (This is why they need a girlfriend!) When they are tired and hungry after work, many guys go solo when dining out at restaurants. So if you want to meet a new man, try a new restaurant at least once a week. Or become a regular at one of your favorites. Don't think of dining for one as a lonely number. It is an approachable number, and makes you easier to talk to. Plus, it gives you a day off in the kitchen. Consider it your once-a-week treat. If you're concerned about being alone and bored, bring along a book or a magazine to keep you occupied.

8. Hit the Gym. Getting in shape alongside hot guys with hard bodies. 'Nuf said.

9. Let Your Doggie Do It. A dog can be woman's best friend when it comes to meeting men, says askmen.com. But don't take Fido for just any old walk—bring him to the local dog park for a more social stroll. That way, while the pooch plays with his new pals, you can make a few of your own. Meanwhile, many entrepreneurs are finding that our four-legged friends are natural-born matchmakers. Online social clubs like New York–based Leashes and Lovers host cocktail parties for single dog owners to connect—and share photos of their pets.

10. Host a Shindig. Throwing a party is one of the best ways to get into the dating scene, according to ladieshomejournal .com. Theme parties, a Halloween costume ball, or an Academy Awards bash, are always easygoing affairs where people really get into the spirit of the celebration. Have your guests bring a friend you've never met, and even if you don't meet an eligible bachelor at your own shindig, becoming the hostess-with-the-mostest will naturally get you reciprocally invited to other events where you might meet your some kind of wonderful.

11. Fly the Friendly Skies. The next time you have a flight, look out for cute guys who might also be flying on the same plane. And if you're on Southwest where you can choose your own seat, who knows, maybe you'll able to get a seat right next to his!

12. Be Politically Active. Become a part of something you believe in, whether it's the Save Darfur Coalition or the Red Cross, where you can meet smart, passionate guys who do good by helping others. Find your favorite cause, and check the calendar for upcoming rallies, vigils, roundtables, and concerts. Or become a party animal and join a political campaign. The best part: Many senatorial and gubernatorial campaign teams are male-dominated, and the atmosphere can be intense. According to cosmopolitan.com, these live-for-the-moment occasions are also ripe for making love connections.

13. Read Between the Lines. Really into body art? Let your love of tattoos and body piercings lead you to your like-minded mate. Whether you're into permanent inkings, or wear-and-wash, TatooedSingles.com is a free site offering men and women with designs on dating a carefree environment in which to navel gaze (and, in this case, if there's a diamond stud in there, that's not such a bad thing) or connect with your soul mate.

14. Choose Wine, Not Whining. Are you a lover of great wine? Then whisk yourself off to the Ellis House Wine Camp on the east end of Long Island, New York, for a three-night stay. Recommended by naturalhealthmag.com, the four-day behind-the-scenes tour with winemakers and private tastings. And if you meet a fellow connoisseur, you can stroll the quaint villages and beaches in the area . . . hand-in-hand. Awww.

15. Share Social Experiences With Other Singles. Hiking, volleyball, theatre outings, kayaking, dance lessons: just a handful of activities offered by social clubs like Highlight Adventures. Located in Chicago, Indianapolis, Los Angeles, and

Orange County, these membership-only groups organize professionally planned activities for singles that promise to promote a fun, relaxed atmosphere in which to meet new people, find friendship, or connect with that special someone. Many conduct background checks before accepting new clients. And be prepared for an initiation meeting where you will be asked to fill out plenty of paperwork on your interests and expectations.

16. Step Outside Your Comfort Zone. Girls who look like Gidget are not the only ones who can hang ten. You can learn how to ride the waves at local surf camps in your area. Or head to the shores in Southern California or Costa Rica to enroll in Surf Diva's two- or five-day women-only camp sessions taught by world-class surfers, where you can connect with your inner soul surfer, while looking oh-so-svelte in your beach babe gear. Not a water woman? Not a problem. Try tapping into your inner cowgirl for some horseback riding on a working cattle ranch, or glide through the air while ziplining in Hawaii. Releasing your inhibitions in one area of your life may help you open up in others.

17. Go On, Get Fresh. A growing number of us are becoming more concerned about the foods we eat and are turning our attention to locally grown, organic foods and farmers' markets are blooming with healthy choices and men of discerning taste. While health-food chains like Whole Foods Market and Trader Joe's may carry a larger supply of good-for-you foods, and national chains like Target, Walmart, and Safeway are now offering pesticide-free organics and nutritious packaged goods, a local farmers' market offers a more intimate setting in which to get to know the vendors—and regular shoppers. Be consistent, and you may find you'll be squeezing more than just peaches.

18. Biking Is Cool. Even in my native Los Angeles, home to bazillions of cars, bike riding is becoming a hip mode of transportation. And all over the country, biking clubs are offering two-wheelers a chance for weekend—and weekday—rides. If you prefer a bike with more horsepower, get on a hog. Trade in your business suit for a little leather and join a motorcycle club where you can meet other weekend warriors who keep day jobs as business owners and heads of Fortune 500 companies.

19. Consult a Pro. Matchmakers are not just characters found in *Fiddler on the Roof.* There are individual matchmakers, as well as companies, that set people up. One of the more popular services, It's Just Lunch, sets up dates for busy professionals to meet over a casual brunch, lunch, or just drinks. They do all the work setting up the place and coordinating schedules, and you just show up and enjoy the date.

20. Weddings Aren't Always About the Bride and Groom. Yes, weddings are an occasion to celebrate a marriage between two formerly single people, but it's also an opportunity for you to mingle with new ones notes ehow.com. But don't go giving your phone number to a potential date during the ceremony. Wait until the reception, where you'll have plenty of time to approach someone you think is attractive, or be approached by someone smitten with you. And don't forget to check out who's lining up for the garter toss: a happy band of single boys just waiting to be beaus.

21. Reunions Connect More Than Old Classmates. Reunions are also some of the best places to reconnect with those you haven't seen in a long time, and meet someone you may not have previously known. Perhaps the guy you had a crush on in high school is now single and looking for someone just like you. Or, maybe that guy who you would never have given the time of day is now someone you might consider sharing an afternoon.

22. RSVP to That Next Social Event. Don't toss that invitation to your friend's housewarming, birthday party, or coed baby shower. You never know who you might meet. These kinds of social outings are often some of the easiest places to find a potential mate because guests are generally encouraged to get to know each other. Since there might not be much else to do other than socialize, it presents a viable opportunity to strike up a conversation with a fellah you fancy.

23. Take In Some Culture. Sidewalk art shows, a classic pianist performance, a nationally renowned public speaker, or the Russian ballet make for wonderful opportunities for mind-expanding ideas and entertainment, while putting you in a prime position for bumping into your Mr. Right (or Mr. Right, Right Now). You can invite a family member, friend, or coworker to go along, but showing up solo may make you more accessible—and approachable. Either way, be open to meeting new people, whether it's the person in the next seat or getting into a conversation with an intriguing someone during intermission.

24. Scope Out the Neighborhood. Join your community block club, especially if you're new to an area. Then keep your eyes peeled during the next block party for someone you might not have met yet. Community garage sale coming up? Go check it out. It may be that there is someone who shares your interests in antique toys, or others that are just interesting. Getting to know your neighbors can open you up to more social opportunities, and it's a great way to take your time and observe how someone lives on a day-to-day basis before you decide to embark on a dating relationship.

25. Become a Volunteer. Helping others is definitely good karma: the love you give just might come right back to you. Choose causes that speak to your heart, whether it is for children, the homeless, animals, AIDS prevention, or your religious affiliation. Studies show that people who volunteer have fewer incidents of depression and higher self esteem. Volunteering is a great way to feel like you serve a purpose in the world and a great way to meet people. Online organizations like Volunteer Match could help you find an organization you will be excited to help. You could find that your passion is shared by someone who wants to be passionate with you.

26. Check Out a Museum Exhibit. Museums have special events and members-only affairs. Become a member and meet lots of intriguing, cultured people.

27. Hit the Sporting Events. Enjoy a good game of football? Maybe soccer or basketball? Professional sporting events, and even amateur ones, are guaranteed to be fun and you can find men of all kinds.

28. Find a Flea Market. People watching is just as much fun as browsing for kitschy finds.

29. Join a Coed Book Club. Check your local library for book club and other mind-stimulating events. You can always start your own group. Some local bookstores have community bulletin boards where you can post meetings. Then see who shows up. Reading books and sharing them is another great way to get to know men who might make potential partners.

30. Engage in Extended Family Activities. This probably seems like a weird one, and it may not be your cup of tea, but hanging out with my brother and his family at my niece's pee-wee league baseball games or school recitals are great ways to meet single uncles who are out supporting their respective nieces or nephews. Getting to know more of the friends and co-workers of your siblings, and even cousins, opens your meeting potential even more.

31. Start Your Own Social Club. Don't wait around for someone else to initiate the next great social group. Try starting one yourself. Being the "organizer" can bring a boost to your social life. Try planning a weekly movie night with your friends, and ask them to invite their friends along, and see who shows up each week. Make it clear that new people are welcome to join at any time.

32. Try Random Acts of Fun. Grab the local free paper or go to Craigslist.com and check out the section with a list of events that are happening that week. Then go. It may be a bust or you just may meet someone you like.

33. Grab a Cup o' Joe. Coffee shops are great place to engage with men. Many creative types tend to camp out at local watering holes and work on projects. But try not to immerse yourself in something so completely that you send off those "I'm too busy to deal" vibes notes about.com. You want to be inviting, and hiding behind a laptop or a 300-page novel isn't a great "come hither" opportunity. (Although you might want to just keep a copy of *Swirling* on the table as a conversation starter . . . who knows?) Smile and say hello, and make yourself available for that tête-à-tête, be it a recommendation for a new book to read, a compliment about something you're wearing, or maybe even a date. Sure, someone might not speak back when spoken to. But ten seconds later, another one walks through the door. There's nothing lost in the process. Because opening up enables you to gain so much more.

34. Exercise Your High IQ. Intellectual singles are increasingly meeting their high-IQ matches at events geared toward people looking to exercise their minds. Are you a Mensa member? Check for parties in your area. Enjoy scavenger hunts? Watson Adventures hosts hunts at museums, zoos, circuses, and other interesting places in cities such as New York, San Francisco, Seattle, and Boston.

35. Make Some Home Improvements. A recent perusal of the Guy Talk board on iVillage.com finds Home Depot a great man-meeting spot, with available guys roaming the aisles for tools, fixtures, wood—and dates with self-reliant, do-it-themselves kind of gals. The stores also offer classes on home repair and construction projects.

36. Sports Bars Are Still Where Men Hang Out. If you're a sports-loving woman, you can always find nice sports-loving men congregating at a cocktail lounge, tavern, or pub where there is a big game on TV. If you don't find a compatible mate, you can at least have a cheap evening out. Often the bars will offer free drinks to women on those nights.

37. Learn the Art of Public Speaking. You can boost your career skills and meet interesting people at the same time through such public speaking organizations such as Toastmasters. And it's free!

38. Attend a Trade Show. Love cars? Boats? Or other adult toys? Trade shows are a great place to get lots of free information, goodies, and maybe even a date. Your city's convention center will have a calendar of scheduled events.

39. Train For a Marathon. This is one of the best ways I've found to meet men. While trekking the miles during my training for two marathons in Los Angeles, I would often see the same run/walk enthusiasts who traveled along the same path. Familiarity soon brought a smile, then a "Hello" . . . and several times I got asked out on dates. Mostly my walks were solo. But there are also groups like the LA Leggers and the LA Road-runners, where you can meet other hoofers. Plus, they'll teach people how to train for the event, organize group runs, and host guest speakers.

40. Have an Apple. Believe it or not, cosmopolitan.com recommends The Apple store as a place to meet men. I decided to see for myself. On a recent trip to the land of iPods and Mac-Books in Santa Monica, there were indeed an overwhelming number of men shopping for gadgets at the boutiques—and the vibe at these stories are conducive to man meeting, too. I found I could get plenty of assistance from men more than willing to help this technophobe in distress. You can also take free workshops on anything from Photoshop to podcasting—another great opportunity to strike up a conversation. Or just hang out and pursue all the good-looking (nonmechanical) merchandise. Plus, there are more than 200 Apple stores (and counting) in 42 states. Chances are, there is one close by where you live.

41. Live Abroad for a Year. Films like *Under the Tuscan Sun* and *Eat Pray Love* have many of us yearning for exotic, faraway places with dashing international lovers. Getting out of dodge can certainly provide you with a new perspective on life, along with new mating possibilities. It's best to take a vacation to the country you're interested in before packing up everything for twelve months or more. And learn the language *before* you go. Once you find out what people are really saying about you, you might have a different opinion of the place you have chosen, notes friend and author Kelly E. Carter, who lived in Italy for a year and is writing a book, *Bellini for One*, about her experience. "Learn what is acceptable for women in the country you are moving to and adapt," Kelly advises. "And be flexible. Moving to a country like Italy, where being a singleton past the age of twenty-five is frowned upon, makes it very hard to find single men to date." So, if you're over thirty, be willing to date down.

42. Take a Walk in the Park. A brisk stroll is heart smart . . . in more ways than one.

43. Cooking Is a Great Way to Start, *Ahem*, Cooking. Whether you are a novice or an expert, there's nothing that heats things up between a man and a woman quite like cooking together. "Everybody loves food—and although a lot of guys don't cook, more men are signing up for classes because *they* know that's where women are," says Tracey Augustine, chef and proprietor of Cashmere Bites, an exotic creative culinary studio in Los Angeles. The culinary studio offers classes for groups of twelve to sixteen, and special events and parties are always on the menu. Cookware boutique Sur la Table also offers how-tos for budding at-home chefs in their regional stores across fifteen states, and well as culinary vacations in New York and Italy.

44. Learn a New Language. Spanish, Italian, Portuguese, Latin, and French: they don't call them romance languages for nothing.

45. Join a Sports Team. You don't have to be an Olympic athlete to try out for a team. Local YMCAs and recreational centers welcome active participants for baseball, volleyball, swimming, and other sporting leagues where you can engage with a fellow player one-on-one, or maybe even garner a fan (or two) of your own.

46. Be At the Head of the Class. Teach something in which you are an expert. In a down economy, a side gig is always useful, and allows you to meet interesting grown-ups. Offer seminars on your subject to expand your network . . . and potential dates.

47. Karaoke Amateur Night. Tap into your inner Mary J. Blige and hit a few high notes at an area karaoke spot. And don't be afraid to let your hair down a little and shake your groove thing for your adoring audience. Trust me: it will be "just fine."

48. Body Building Can Boost More Than Muscle. Inspired by seventy-four-year-old amateur body builder Ernestine Shepherd, a silver-haired sister who holds the Guinness Book record for oldest female body builder, I had to add this to the list. Not only will you get comfortable in your body pumping all that iron, you can also boost your self-esteem while competing in events that often have bleachers brimming with men.

49. Point and Shoot. As a devoted shutterbug since high school, photography is a great way to scope out and find interesting new subjects—including men. Besides my salt and pepper hair, and youthful face, which often leads to instant inquiries from men (and, well, women, too), being behind the lens of my 35mm Canon XE is always a for sure conversation starter.

50. Put On Your Dancing Shoes. Learn to salsa, rumba, cha-cha, tango, or even ballroom dance. And for this closet country girl, square dancing is a real hoot and a holler. Dance has really come to the forefront in recent years, thanks in part to the popularity of reality shows like *Dancing with the Stars* and *So You Think You Can Dance*. Not only is dancing fun and a great way to exercise, it allows you to get close to your partner. Dance classes are now filling up all over the country, and you can choose pay-as-you-go classes, or sign up for an extended period of time (some classes can be up to eight weeks). For the best opportunities to meet eligible guys, choose singles classes, and check to make sure no partner is required. Plus, knowing how to dance makes you popular at social events, like weddings, reunions, and other special occasions.

51. Professional Networking Events. Beyond shaking hands and passing out business cards, you can meet a lot of really cute single professionals. Shakers and Stirrers, a monthly after-hours mixer in Santa Monica, caters to businesspeople looking to make contacts. As it was, I sealed a deal that led to an ongoing love affair. Check out my afterword in the back of the book if you want the whole story.

52. Go to the Hair Salon. Depending on where you get your hair *did,* you might not meet a straight date *in* the beauty shop. But once you step out, girl . . . watch the heads turn. (Then give a little smile and wave as you whip your head back and forth.) Whether you like your hair au naturel; close cropped; in freshly twisted locks; fried, dyed, and laid; or, like me, in God-given shimmery gray, a great cut and style will always show your outward confidence and great looks, and make you ready for when someone notices your beauty within.

CHAPTER NINE

Janice

The Rules of Flirtation: Knowing When He's Interested

flirt > *v. 1. [intrans.] behave as though attracted to or trying to attract someone, but without serious intention*

—THE OXFORD AMERICAN COLLEGE DICTIONARY, 2002

He fell in love with her writing before he met her. But when journalist Steve Korris finally got around to inviting fellow reporter Linda Lockhart to dinner, she had no idea he was making his move on her. It was the late 1960s, and Steve was the only white reporter working at the *St. Louis American,* the local black weekly. Linda, who is black, covered similar stories for the mainstream daily paper, the *St. Louis Post Dispatch.* "I didn't enjoy most of the reporters who wrote for the *Post Dispatch*—I thought there was a lot arrogance in their writing, a lot of condescension, showing off," Steve says. "Linda's stories were always straight down the line, very compact, very direct, and I appreciated that, and she stood out in my mind for that reason." Steve would often run into Linda while the two were on assignment; they even shared the stage a couple of times on panels for local public television. "And then one Sunday, I covered an event while she was on her regular full shift," Steve recalls, "and when the event was over, I asked, 'Can I kind of just follow you around?' And we had so much fun that day while she continued her work that as she drove away, I had this feeling like I don't want this to end, and so got a little more direct. I called and asked her to dinner." (Linda, over the phone from their home in St. Louis, begins to laugh: "I didn't know he was asking me out on a *date!*")

Linda, like Steve, was divorced. Neither had ever dated outside their race, and it never occurred to Linda that Steve was even remotely interested. She didn't recognize the signals he says he had been giving out—until he came to pick her up. "We were supposed to meet at six o'clock," Linda continues, "and he walked into the newsroom about a quarter to, and I looked up and I said, 'Oh gee, I wish my dates were so punctual!' and I could tell by the look on his face he was hurt, and I thought, *Oh, he thinks this is a date.* Right then it was a whole different ballgame."

Although Steve had been neither overt nor aggressive, just wanting to be around Linda, now his wife of thirty years and the mother of their two adult children, was his way of breaking the ice and making his intentions known. Only Linda had no idea what was on his mind.

Want to know what a guy is really thinking? Truth be told, most women do—it would make this whole relationship thing so much easier. There are lots of ways to decipher what a man wants by the way he flirts. Many of us think of flirting as the overly aggressive, annoying pickup lines: *Hey baby, what's your phone number?* That kind of talk might be amusing in quippy '80s pop songs, but let's not get it twisted: that's antagonistic, sexual-harassment-lawsuit kind of behavior, not a courtship maneuver. And flirting isn't all talk. It extends to gestures, body language, eye movement, and attentiveness, what scientists call "contact readiness cues," which are common to the relationship initiation processes.

Why We Flirt

Flirting is as natural as blinking, and most of the time we don't even realize we're doing it. We're hardwired that way, and we often give off signs that we have an interest in someone almost before we consciously have a say in it. The slightest movements reveal so much: like the times you smile and laugh at his joke even though he is not all that funny. Or how you tilt your head just so to expose a little bit of your neck; the way you move in closer to him to hear his every single word. The slightest raise of your eyebrow or mimicking his actions or gestures: These are all typical indicators that tell the other person you're ready to engage physically, and more important, that you're not intending to run away from him. (For men, the message is that he's not planning to be dominating or threatening.) The biology part of this is well documented. According to Belinda Luscombe, in her *TIME* magazine article on the science of romance, ethologist Irenäus Eibl-Eibesfeldt, then of the Max Planck Institute in Germany, filmed African tribes in the 1960s and found that the women there did the exact same prolonged stare followed by a head tilt away with a little smile that he saw in America. Nature has her way of bringing us together.

And, yes, birds and bees do it, too. It is why some males birds have exotic plumage, why elk carry hefty antlers (a sign of a healthy immune system—now you *know* that's sexy), why a male fiddler crab has enormous claws, which enables him to wave and alert female crabs of his whereabouts, and then invite them to come closer for a better look at his burrow, his colorful shell, and his big member. (And, yes, I'm referring to his claw . . . what were *you* thinking?) All mammals have their ways of signaling surrender and, as humans, flirting allows us to open up the physical and verbal lines of communications and puts us on even playing fields.

Just know that the endgame might be very different. While it is not always a precursor to sex—although rest assured, ladies, for men sex is most often always the goal—flirting can be a default mechanism to score a free drink, to get a better table, to get cutsies in a line at the supermarket, or to get out of a speeding ticket. (C'mon, you know you've tried it!)

Signals change in the digital arena where it's all about words, and no body language. Whether it's online on social media sites, in chat rooms, on Internet dating pages or text messaging, understanding the nuances are almost impossible to detect. Flirting via text or e-mail often moves things forward faster. Because there is no face-to-face, or eye-to-eye contact, people are often less inhibited and more willing to disclose intimate details about themselves that are bolder and racier than would be revealed during in-person dialogue.

Monique Neal, a thirty-nine-year-old paralegal—and my second cousin on my dad's side—met her husband, Barry, a white, forty-five-year-old elevator technician, ten years ago online after she placed an ad on the website for *Blind Date*, a syndicated TV reality show that was on the air from 1999 to 2006, pairing perfect strangers and sending them off on their blind date with cameras following their every move. "I think I placed the ad on campus, sometime between classes," says Monique, who, at the time was juggling work and a full class schedule at California State University, Dominguez Hills. She had totally forgotten about the ad when, one night after work, she came home to find an e-mail from Barry in response to her ad. "I read the e-mail, and Barry described himself, and then he wrote, 'If you want to talk, e-mail me back and I'll send you my phone number.' And I was like, 'Isn't that strange?'" she says with a sly smile. "But I was really intrigued because everything he said made me think that it wasn't a joke, 'cause you know how you get those jokey emails, and I e-mailed him back and sure 'nuf, he sent me his phone number and at work the next day, because I worked at a group home at the time, and while the kids were occupied, I called him." The conversation lasted about three hours. "After we talked that night, that was a Monday, we talked every day since," she says, adding that neither of them had exchanged photographs, although each had described themselves so they knew they were of a different race, and she admits there was lots of on-the-phone flirtiness. "We were definitely flirting with each other, I mean, immediately," she says. "Talking to him on the phone was like talking to someone I'd known forever, just so normal and natural, but it was just the weirdest thing, it was like we were meant to be together." Barry said he wanted to meet. It was just after Thanksgiving. "He came down that weekend and we spent the weekend together. It wasn't love at first sight, like *bam*, it was nothing like that," she says, admitting he looked just the way he described himself, so that wasn't the issue. "We did have to get used to one another, but it didn't take long for us to fall in love with each other, because I knew this was going to be something that would go beyond just the regular boyfriend and girlfriend thing, and we've been together ever since."

Fairfax, California, couple, Robert, a fifty-eight year old white banker, and Jennifer,* a forty-four year old graduate student, on the other hand, met the old-fashioned way: He answered her ad in the personals section of the *San Francisco Weekly*. "Living in San Francisco makes it incredibly difficult to date—there are so many gay men and, it seems, not enough straight ones. I had lots of male friends in San Francisco, but I knew them so well that I wouldn't date any of them: great friends, not good boyfriend material," Jennifer says of her decision to turn to the classifieds. She had dated white, Asian, and Latino men before, so she was open to any possibility; both she and Robert believed they would find real romance. "Oddly enough, my sister also found her husband that way, and I know quite a few people who have met through personal ads and at the time that seemed to be the way that people met each other," she says. "I just thought I'd check it out and see what happened," says Robert, admitting he was deliberately looking for an African American woman. He'd been married before, to a white woman, but had always been attracted the "exotic beauty" of black women, but more than that, he says, was intrigued by this woman who, on paper, loved Merlot, Chopin, and reading the Sunday *New York Times*. "She even mentioned smoking cigars occasionally, which I don't smoke and never will, but I found that quite interesting, and her age was just right. She was obviously an intelligent person based on the ad she put together." A phone conversation ensued, "and we liked each other immediately when we realized we had so many things in common, and I don't remember how many conversations we had on the phone before we met," she says, and he adds, "It was just a couple. We started talking about books right away and how we both like books, how we had so many books, and how it's hard to throw books away, it was just a good connection." Both, however, contend there wasn't a lot of intentional flirtatiousness going on in their conversation. "Jennifer is not the flirty type," Robert says.

There is no shame in a little good-natured flirting. It opens us up to the potential for something to happen, allowing us a peak at what could be, with the option, if we choose, to close the door: no harm, no foul.

When Danielle Milton e-mailed me about her dating experi-

> There is no shame in a little good-natured flirting. It opens us up to the potential for something to happen.

ences, I immediately related to her story of having met and dated a white man she had met on an airplane. I'd had a long-distance fling for nearly a year with a white guy from Bozeman, Montana, whom I had met while on a United flight from New York to Las Vegas.

For her part, Danielle, a twenty-eight year old CPA from Kansas City, Missouri, was on a two-hour commuter flight from Detroit to Maine, eventually heading to New Hampshire on an assignment, when a man, on his cell phone, boarded the aircraft, one of those small, narrow-body cabins with two seats on each side of the aisle, and sat next to her. "I was seated on the outer seat, and this guy came in and he was at the window seat so I had to get up to let him in, and I noticed he was very well built, and he was extremely tanned," she begins. "I thought he may have been Hispanic or something because he didn't look white, he was *that* tan—and he was talking and kept mentioning Kansas as he was on the phone, and I thought, hmmm, that's really weird, another person with a connection to Kansas.

"After he hung up, I said, 'Hey! I heard you mentioning Kansas. Are you from there? I'm from Kansas City,'" she recalls, "and we just began to talk, and I came to find out that his family is from rural Kansas. He had just been there to help with the harvest, and we just started talking about a bunch of different things. His family also owned a lobster business in Maine, which is where he lived permanently." At some point he asked what she did for a living. "I told him I was a CPA, and he started telling me about how he wanted to buy the lobster business from his father and how they had been dealing with these auditors and asking for my professional opinion and experience on some things." From there, the conversation segued into politics and the current financial culture. "I work for H&R Block Bank, I manage their internal audit department," Danielle continues, "and he used to work in an H&R Block tax office, so there was just a lot we had in common, and I told him I was going to Intervale, New Hampshire, to the tax office there, and we exchanged contact information."

Danielle and Mr. Kansas had a few conversations while they were in the area, she says, "and then right before I was leaving, he picked me up from the airport—and I took appropriate safety precautions," she says, noting that she had alerted airline personnel of her rendezvous in case she didn't return for her flight. "And we went to the downtown port in Maine.

"It was so much fun. I found out then that he was a little younger than me, he was like twenty-three or twenty-four, and as it turned out he hadn't finished college yet and he felt like he was behind his peers, even though he had been helping to run two businesses for his family, but I could tell he had some apprehension about that, and there were some other things, too, but I kind of took the experience for what it was worth. It was just great to meet someone and have a meaningful connection even if it doesn't go anywhere romantically."

No harm. No foul.

Knowing The Signs

Judging from the scores of interviews conducted for this book, along with the comments posted on *Beyond Black & White*, black women typically say they can often tell when a black man is flirting, an assumption that has some basis in truth. It goes back to that social distance idea: there is a sense of familiarity among most African Americans. It is why we tend to gravitate toward one another at work functions when there is only one or two of us in a room full of people of other races; why black men, perfect strangers, greet one another with a nod while walking down the street and know they're in good company; why we call ourselves "brother" and "sister" as terms of endearment even though we are not blood related. Our black is our bond. There is, however, no scientific evidence to support the assumption that African American men actually behave any differently than a rainbeau-American in how he approaches a black woman—it's all in how *we* process it.

At the time I spoke to Lauren and Adam,* both work in insurance and risk management, they were just a couple months away from tying the knot. The two met while at an out-of-town risk management conference, and had been invited to some of the same functions, and a broker client introduced them to one another. But Lauren had no clue that Adam was remotely interested. "It was funny—I had dated interracially before, but it had been a long, long time, and so I didn't catch the cues immediately that he liked me," she says. The two started chatting it up at the conference, "because you do so much talking at conferences," Lauren says. They both lived in Fort Worth, Texas, and their offices were very close to each other. "We decided we would go out to lunch when we got back," Adam begins, "and when we got back I asked her out to lunch, per our agreement, and she stalled. It became kind of this cat and mouse thing, but she finally acquiesced."

The lunches became more frequent over the next several months, but Lauren still wasn't getting it. "It was really a girlfriend of mine who worked close by, and usually she and I would go out to lunch together several days a week," says Lauren. "She starts noticing that she's getting stood up for several lunches and she said, 'You know what? I think he likes you,' and I was like, 'No, no, we're just friends. We're just having lunch.' But she was the one who finally pointed out, 'I think he likes you.' And when I kind of opened myself up to that, then I was like, 'Yeah, and I think I like him too.'"

The problem that most black women have is recognizing when a nonblack fellah is showing he is interested. That, says experts in the field, is because detecting flirtatious behavior is dependent on three things: 1. the goal of the sender, 2. the goal of the receiver, and 3. the responses of the *receiver* to those actions. To put it another way, you only recognize that a man is flirting with you if you think he's flirting. The problem that most women have when dating out is the assumption that different rules apply, says David Dryden Henningsen, PhD, associate professor of communications theory at Northern Illinois University in DeKalb. "Sometimes that's the great deniability of flirting behaviors, because the more uncertain you are about the person, the less likely you are to consider it flirting," he says. "So the likelihood of misinterpretation or understanding of the person's intent becomes greater when you step outside of your race or culture because there are uncertainties of specific behaviors and how we can interpret it."

Here are a few obvious tell-tell indicators to help you pick up on the signals:

Eye contact. Whether it's a lingering stare from across a room or a park, or if his glance grabs your attention for more than an accidental moment and he smiles, he's definitely interested.

Compliments. Doesn't matter if it's your toenail polish or your hair, he's noticing things about you and pay close attention to the things he likes about you.

Focus. Chances are if he's engaged with you, rather than scanning everything that moves in the room, he's totally flirting with you.

Touch. If he briefly puts his hand on yours when you tell a funny story, or puts a hand on your shoulder when he asks if you want another drink, know he's interested.

Attention. When it's all about you, and he's asking personal questions to draw out more information about you, he's likely seeking a deeper connection.

Made In ~~America~~ _____?

Now if we were only focusing on men of Western culture and upbringing, we'd be pretty much done at this point. The problem that most women have when dating an ethnic man, the cues could be even more difficult to detect, ambiguities in intent that are inherent and ripe for misinterpretation. "There is certainly a lot of evidence that there are differences in nonverbal cues [across varying cultures]," says Dr. Henningsen. A common example of that, he says, would be interpersonal space. In some cultures some people will stand much closer to you in general, without it being interpreted as intimate. However, in Western cultures we tend to give each other a little more space—unless we're wanting to, well, get close. So if the distance between two people is considered a flirting cue "and I stand closer to you, then you could interpret that as a flirting behavior or as a courting initiation—type of behavior," Henningsen offers. Just know, nonverbal communication is also non-symbolic which means it's open to your own interpretation.

In his now well-regarded theory on cognitive valence, San Diego researcher Peter Andersen, PhD, says culture, even more than color differences, play a very definitive role in how men of other cultures interact socially with women. In his research, he offers that, in some cultures, it is permissible to hold hands publicly while in other cultures such open displays of affection are forbidden. Looking at or gazing upon another is accepted, while in other cultures, the eyes are not to be directed at anyone outside your family. Public affection is acceptable in one country, but to kiss touch or hold someone's hand is blasphemous. Even recognizing verbal cues can be convoluted when the ethnic man is from a culture where the social mores dictate that he keep his feelings to himself.

"When you are dating someone from a totally different culture than yours, you have to understand that they do things differently," says thirty-six year old New Yorker and single mother Onica Cupido, an accounting assistant who also runs a blog, *Euphoria Luv,* where she raises awareness for and about black and Asian families, and is editor of The Mommy Factor, where she is often discussing the parenting issues involving her three-year-old son, whose father is Korean. Cupido frequently dates Asian men, and was once married to a man from China. "Within the Chinese culture, things are very different. We are so use to talking about things all the time, versus Chinese people who don't talk about things as openly. They're more action kind of people, like he would do something for me and expect me to understand that it meant he was being affectionate and I didn't get it. Or when he was upset about something, I would say: Why can't you just say what it is? Or, if you don't want me to do something, why can't you just say, 'I would prefer that you didn't do that.' But the thing was that he expected that I should have known by his actions, and I didn't get that. So that was a very big issue for us, because communication is very big in a marriage, and if you have two different communicating styles, you're going to run into it. I did not know that."

Communication differences were a big deal for Nicole Elgh, whose husband, Mathias, is Swedish. "Mathias can be very taciturn and I guess, for everyone else, I'm just a typical American who's just constantly trying to fill the silence," says Nicole, who met the then twenty-two-year-old art student in 1996 on an English-speaking Swedish chat room. At the time, she was twenty, and also an art student, living in Los Angeles. She was planning a trip to Sweden and was hoping to make a few friends before she arrived. On her first log-in, she met Mathias who was living in Seattle, Washington, on a student visa. They hit it off immediately. "We were both a little nuts, and I think we could relate to each other well versus the normals, which was everyone else," Nicole laughs. "It started off personal right away, and once we started talking, I don't think we even talked about Sweden. After a month and a half of regular online and telephone dates, Nicole agreed to meet Mathias in the Emerald City. With the exception of him being over an hour late picking her up from the airport, their first day together was something out of a storybook romance. He was the perfect height, dressed just the way Nicole liked, and "he was aesthetically pleasing," she says. "I thought she was really pretty," Mathias says via Skype from Sweden. They went to see *Blade Runner*, the director's cut, and later went to a Greek diner on Broadway. The whole weekend, Nicole says she was throwing out signals—but it was Mathias who wasn't picking up on the signs.

"He wouldn't make a move, or so I thought," Nicole says of wanting Mathias to finally kiss her. "And I guess I was pushing it, like 'C'mon, we've got to get some action going on here,' and I was trying to test his limits or his boundaries. So I put his hair up in two ponytails and was feeding him candy and I thought, God, what am I going to have to do to get this guy to break through, you know, not breaking the ice because we were already comfortable with each other, but I really wanted him to kiss me and I thought if I initiated something, break down more barriers, that maybe he could become more comfortable and maybe he would, and I finally said, 'Okay, I'm going to give you I don't know how much warning, and then I'm going to kiss you."

What she didn't know, that she later learned studying surveys and reading message boards, articles and blogs with women talking on the subject: Swedish men typically do not make the first move. "I don't know, I mean, I've been with other Swedish women . . . I guess they made the first move" says Mathias, then he giggles. "I guess the way that I am, that that's a typical Swedish trait, I always thought it was something that was typical me. I guess I just thought it was me being insecure and shy."

It's Okay: Make Your Move

With the ambiguities of who's wooing who, it is not unusual these days in a multiethnic relationship for the woman to make the first move. Devra* remembers a lot of friendly flirting when she first met her former fiancé, Simon, a white man whom she dated for eighteen years; although getting him to ask her out on their first date was like trying to get somewhere fast during rush hour: absolutely impossible. He was new to her small suburban town in Massachusetts, and both being creative people, they had a lot in common. "We came from very similar backgrounds," says Devra, a musician who grew up in a suburb just west of Boston. "At the time there were two other black families who lived in a different part of town but I didn't know them. He grew up in a suburb of Detroit. His parents were in a similar social economic class as my parents, although they probably did a little better than my parents did, but we went to the same kind of high school and went to the same kind of college, we like the same kind of music—it wasn't like I listened to Public Enemy and he listened to Barry Manilow—race wasn't really an issue because we spoke the same language." She thought he was cute, kind of dorky, "and he would often ask me, like, 'Oh what are you doing this weekend?' I thought whatever my answer would be that he would say: We should do x, y, and z, and ask me out on a date." But he never did. "And the minute he stopped exhibiting interest, I asked *him* out. It was classic, like when they stop paying attention, it's like 'Wait a minute, what's wrong with me?' I'm not sure that I actually did know that he was interested, but when it seemed like he wasn't anymore, it made me mad, so I asked him on a date. You're not going to get anywhere in life waiting. I certainly haven't."

He's Just That Into You

Like Devra, I have a hard time knowing when a guy is interested in me because I'm such a friendly outgoing person, and typically when you meet a like-minded guy, it's a little difficult to discern if he's mirroring your friendliness or your flirtatious behavior. But generally speaking, when a guy is interested in you romantically, it's usually pretty obvious says Timothy Perper. An independent sex researcher who has been studying flirting since 1978, he notes: "If you ask people who have been in long-term relationships, what you find is that there are these repeated interactions, each of which tests the water a little bit each time to make sure it's safe," Perper says.

That Simon continued to engage with Devra—inquiring about what she liked to do, wanting to hang out and continuing conversations with her; essentially dipping his toe into the shallow end before taking the big plunge. Even though Devra eventually decided to ask him out, they had both waded long enough (and forgive this indulgent extension on the metaphor) that each knew they were okay to dive in. "They're discovering whether they can trust the other one, and sometimes we keep going, and sometimes it isn't [safe]," Perper offers, "and we cut bait and drop back."

Most of the interactions we have in person, rather than those that start online, "are very slow, very cautious," continues Perper. "This is particularly true of men. Most men, not all, know that they should not ogle or touch a woman they've just met, but some of them do. And most men will not touch a woman even after she has touched him. He won't do it. It's too risky emotionally and in terms of social rules, and this can drive women crazy. But it's real."

There is no formula. The answers are not conclusive. ("If I knew the secret, I'd be sitting on the sidelines surrounded by people feeding me Mities," Perper jokes.) In the end, it all depends on the individual. What starts off very mild can ultimately lead to marriage . . . and sometimes not, Perper says. But learning more about cultural mores, and paying attention, can help you assess whether a man might have romantic intentions—and it's that *might*, the uncertainty, that makes it exciting.

So start taking notice of how often the East Indian IT cutie goes out of his way to walk past your desk every morning. Notice how the blond sitting next to you on the airplane leans forward every time you utter a word. Or how the guy behind you in the checkout lane smiles at you, then puffs up his chest a bit—a sure sign he's open and ready for anything you have to throw at him, including a friendly "hello." And who knows, with that maybe step, you can move into the next phase of desire and allure. Neither promises anything more than the invitation to keep it going, and if there is any single component to the art of flirting it's the potential to continue in this delightful interaction that could lead to that first date—where more flirting can, and often does, ensue.

CHAPTER TEN

Janice

The First Date: Finding Neutral Ground

It was not a pretty scene.

A black woman shows up on her first date *ever* with a white guy—having abandoned her cute red dress and peek-toe heels on the advice of her East Indian best friend, who considers herself an interracial dating expert and insisting that white guys like their ladies "casual"—wearing gym shorts and a V-neck tee, which turned out to be a little *too* casual to his dapper look, all impressively dressed in a pair of slacks, white dress shirt, and tie, and a slightly updated Mr. Rogers button-up cardigan.

Hmmm...

Instead of the sushi haunt she was told to expect for their evening outing, her date takes her to soul food haven Aunt Kizzie's Back Porch, for dinner, where after the universal stare-down from all the black people in the tiny joint—including the brother with his arm wrapped around a white woman—the two review the menu with her sandy blond-haired suitor suggesting that she try the fried chicken because he thought *she* would like it.

Ooohhh...

Adding insult to a near punch in the face, the surprise "treat" of the evening was not to be the Donald Glover comedy show she had been eagerly wanting to see, but a finger-snap-happy spoken word poetry slam where tirades of black oppression and dysfunctional "coffee and cream" love affairs had them both squirming in their seats.

Yikes!

It was not exactly the slow motion montage to a 1990s pop love song that she had been fantasizing about all morning. But this episode of *The Misadventures of Awkward Black Girl,* a popular online serial from producer, writer, and star Issa Rae, still ends without getting ugly. After each admitted that they may have been trying just a little too hard to create the perfect "black" and "white" date and—turns out they both like sushi and loathe poetry slams—they share a kiss.

There are some people who relish the anticipation of that first date with all its hope and allure of something new, exciting, and potentially worthwhile—kind of like the first day of senior year in high school (you know all you *lived* for was prom night and graduation day) or Christmas Eve night (when you still believed in Santa Claus and had your fingers crossed that he was bringing you that fabulous toy on the top of your wish list because you had been *so* good that year).

I, on the other hand, dread it as much as I did tenth grade

picture day when I had braces and a Jheri curl. And as much as I've now started to enjoy dating again, I know I just overthink the hell out of that first time out with a guy. What should I wear? How should I do my hair? Do I go with open-toed shoes or high heels? Cleavage? (Or more to the point, how do I get some?) If we go out to eat and something gets caught in my teeth, will he tell me or just stare stupidly at me? What will I do if the conversation goes south? Do I need an emergency out? (And what will it be?) Will I talk too much? (Well, duh, Janice, of course you will.)

But for some black women, as it was in Rae's narrative, first date hand wringing can be exacerbated when the man in question is nonblack. Then it's: Will we have anything in common? What will I say if he brings up race or cultural issues? How will he react if people start to stare? Or, oh my God, what if this is nothing more than jungle fever?

"I did have some reservations," says St. Louis journalist Linda Lockhart of her suitor, colleague Steve Korris. "Once I got over the idea that, 'Okay I can go out with a white guy,' I did have some reservations about his motivation, you know, does he have jungle fever? Is he just trying to figure out what it's like to be with a black woman? I kind of held my emotions back for a while just to see if this guy was really sincere, or is this kind of a passing fancy with him? I was kind of nervous in that regard more than anything else.

"I think I may have even come right out and asked that: 'Do you have jungle fever?' laughs Lockhart. "At that time it was a pretty popular term, you know, it was like, what is up with this guy?"

Steve's response: "I remember saying to her, the only way I

can put your mind at ease is to stick around because I had already passed the point of no return."

Establish Common Ground

First dates can be sometimes treacherous enough without all the added extras of holding up the differences of race, culture or religion says New York psychologist Lisa Orbe-Austin, PhD.

No matter who you're dating, you should always focus on commonalities and similarities—and especially for mixed relationships where the obvious differences are around race and ethnicity, you should at least share other things in common: social class, education level, and/or occupation type (i.e., whether it is professional or trade).

> **Especially for mixed relationships where obvious differences are around race and ethnicity, you should share other things in common.**

Even the place you choose for your first date is important. "You want to go somewhere where you're going to be in a mixed crowd because it will allow you to feel like everyone else, which is so important—you want to feel like you're in a comfort zone and not out of place," says Dr. Orbe-Austin. That means no soul food joints in "da hood," or bistros on that side of town where the clientele is sure to be all one type that doesn't look like you. For me, that means no more agreeing to go to Mexican restaurants with Latino men . . . at least not until my Spanish improves. (*What did he just say to that pretty waitress that made her smile like that?*)

The playing field should be level for both you and your partner.

Finding a diverse place for a date is usually easier in larger metropolitan cities like San Francisco, Los Angeles, Minneapolis, Chicago, or New York. But in areas where race is more polarized—say, anywhere in the south with the possible exception of maybe Atlanta—it's best to stay away from a place that is brand-new to either of you. "When you're dating someone, you also need to pay attention to the fact that *they* pay attention to that," Orbe-Austin says. "So if they're taking you out to a place and you don't feel comfortable, that has meaning."

My cousin, Monique Neal, and her husband, Barry, chose Red Lobster: a mutual favorite.

For Fairfax, California, couple Jennifer and Robert*, it was dinner at Savor in San Francisco, a popular laid-back little restaurant in Noe Valley which, according to the site Not For Tourists, attracts a lot of young families, lesbians, and well-heeled ex-hippies.

"Jennifer lived in that neighborhood, and we agreed we'd have dinner there," says Robert. "And since we talked a lot about books, like I said before, I brought her a book and I didn't have a chance to wrap it, and there was a little drugstore nearby the restaurant, so I went in and asked if I could have a bag."

The book: *The Name of the Rose*, Italian author Umberto Eco's much admired 1980s mystery novel involving medieval theology (which was later made into a film starring my forever crush Sean Connery). "There aren't too many guys who would bring a book on a first date," Jennifer gushes. "That really appealed to me, and definitely a very smart thing on his part to do. I had not read the book, and had never even heard of Umberto Eco before, so that was good. And then it was really all about the two of us having a real conversation."

Keep the conversation on the things you have in common, in the same way Jennifer and Robert did. Although they were of different socioeconomic classes and backgrounds, they were similar intellectually. Both had gone to college. Both were working. So their discussion veered on fun, light, wanting-to-get-to-know-more-of-you banter that left them both eager for a second date. As Orbe-Austin points out, you really want to steer clear of any explosive topics that might address racial tensions or differences from the beginning.

And do not, I repeat, *absolutely do not*, inquire whether you are his first black date, or volunteer that this is your first swirl.

"No, oh no, hell no!" Orbe-Austin sternly warns. "You're not looking to have these deep conversations from the beginning. You're looking to build to that place. The relationship at that point cannot tolerate conflict. You don't have enough trust. You don't have enough of a bond with that person to deal with anything that might invoke a conflict. It's really about staying away from any explosive topics that shows you've got issues."

Of course, *he* might be the one with the hang-ups. I'm remembering a particular first date incident while back in undergraduate school at Loyola Marymount University. At the time, I worked part-time as a general merchandise clerk at a now defunct grocery store chain—and was subbing at the Venice Boulevard location over the summer when I met the tall, tanned, dark-haired Caucasian salesman who sold wines to the liquor department. He looked like an athlete that some shaving cream company would put in a commercial bare-chested and lathering up—mind you, this was back in the late 1980s when jocks had to look good in order to get deals on TV. After a couple of weeks of friendly banter, the guy asked me out on a date and, after a customary interrogation from my father when he picked me up from home, he decided to let me know I was *his* first black date . . . and just before we pulled up to the restaurant. Never mind that he proceeded on his true confessions tirade with an admission that his father's mistress, the woman who broke up his parents' marriage of twenty-some years, was black and that, before getting to know me, he would *never* have seen himself going out with a black woman. "I wouldn't want my mom to think I was doing it just because my dad did it—but, of course, you're different."

Nor was I stupid.

Go With the Flow

Indeed, we all have issues. And in some situations, it may be difficult to avoid conversations about race. But do not force the issue. The best way to have the discussion is to let it come out naturally. "You wait until it spontaneously bubbles up," Detroit psychologist Gail Parker, PhD. "If you are so anxious to have the conversation, I guess you can. But it's almost like having the conversation about 'What are your intentions?' up front. That's like asking about marriage on a first date. He doesn't know you yet, so why have that conversation now?"

And for many of the couples that Christelyn and I have spoken with, race is rarely an issue at this point in the relationship. "Basically on our first date, there was never anything about race or anything but what we were looking for in a relationship," says cousin Monique, who had dated white guys in high school and college. Barry's girlfriend before Mo was black. "It wasn't like I was trying to stay away from it, it just wasn't a big deal for either of us. Eventually it came up, like: Have you ever dated a black woman? Have you every dated a white guy? And since we had, it was like, Oh well. Next."

"I'm a firm believer of no games," says Kimberly, the stay-at-home mom from Maryland whose husband, Jonathan, is of Polish and German background. "I'm not saying put everything out there on the first date, but I had dated Asian men mostly, and didn't have a lot of contact with white men in a dating sense, even though I was completely open to it. I'd heard all these things that my sisters would say: Oh white men only use black women for sex. They only go out with light-skinned women. And my older sister, who is light-skinned herself, was saying, 'They'll want me, but they won't want you,' and I was like, *oookaaayyy*! So it was after about a month of dating, I asked him: Hey, where are we going with this? What ride am I on?"

Because they worked in the same field, Lauren and Adam of Fort Worth, Texas, already knew they had that in common. Then over their lunch conversations they learned that they both shared interests in cycling and a fascination for fast cars and other activities, so that by the time they had their first official dinner date, the conversation flowed pretty naturally—and new things about themselves were revealed.

"It's funny, Adam was just so easy to talk to, and we were just talking, and I shared with him that I was Jewish, and he said, 'Wow that's really interesting,' and Adam is Catholic, so it ended up being information he had from the very, very beginning and it adds to our uniqueness, I suppose."

"I was curious about it," Adam says, "and she gave me the story of her conversion and I gave her the story of my conversion . . . "

"Which was something else we had in common," Lauren chimes in, "We were both raised Methodist, he became Catholic and I became Jewish."

Says Adam: "I had never met anybody who had converted to Judaism, and I was a little compelled to find out the thought process behind it, and what drove her, and it was an interesting story that she had about that, and it resonated for me," he says. "I just found it very interesting what you had to go through to convert to the Jewish faith, and then just what it means to be a Jew, that was interesting to me as well. My conversion wasn't on the same level as hers."

As it was, Lauren converted for personal conviction and self-discovery, while Adam became Catholic because, at the time, he was marrying someone in the faith. "I think we related to each other a lot in that," Lauren says, "because in my conversion class there were a lot of people who were there because they were marrying a Jew, and we talked a lot about that and so we also had that in common because it's not an easy journey to take."

Dr. Parker suggests that if the conversation veers toward religion, it definitely should be relevant to the flow of the discussion. "Let's say you're a Christian and you're dating someone who is Muslim. I'm sure there are a lot of curiosities about each other's religious practices, so if it seems natural and normal to bring that up why wouldn't you? But to impose it on the conversation because I'm anxious and in a hurry to find out if we are compatible seems to me to be putting an awful lot of pressure on a relationship that doesn't exist yet. So if this is the first time I'm meeting you and you mention to me, I'm a Muslim or I'm a Christian or whatever, then the response is: Really? I've always been curious about that. Can we have that conversation? Otherwise it's too soon. It's not relevant."

This isn't about negating you or him of your race, ethnicity, or religious beliefs, or relative lack thereof. These are essential to what makes each of you unique, and the elephant that you're obviously bringing to the table, says Parker. "Race and culture are relevant aspects of each person's identity. Hopefully as we're trying to get to know one another—and that's what intimacy is based on, getting to know you—these are discoveries about you, and your partner, that are ongoing. It's not like, 'Okay, now I know this about you,' end of conversation. No. It's an on-going process and how relationships can deepen and continue to grow."

With the tough stuff out of the way, you can relax and enjoy your first rainbeau date. Only one nagging issue to sort out: what to wear. Paging Tim Gunn . . .

CHAPTER ELEVEN

Janice

Moving Forward ... Or Moving On

If there's one thing I've learned about dating, it's that a great first date does not mean the second will be swell. Make it past three weeks, or the next three months, and you could be on your way to something special, but don't go picking out the Lenox wedding china pattern with your rainbeau just yet.

Granted, there are some people who know after the first few dates if it's meant to be, and there are other folks who don't fall in love so easily and need a little more time to sort things through. The last thing you want to do with your mate is to give up on a possible good thing too soon or hold on to a relationship that is not worth your time, and there are ways to tell if the relationship has what it takes to go the distance. "It is very important in the early part of the dating process that you need to notice how they interact with your racial identity and your racial experience," says New York psychologist Lisa Orbe-Austin, PhD. "They don't have to be an expert, but they have to want to learn, and they have to want to make sure you feel comfortable, that you feel safe and that you feel happy. That has to be their priority."

If they can't tolerate when you have racialized experiences— if they're dismissive of anything you might say, like, "Am I being followed by that woman in that store?" and their response is, "No, stop, that's ridiculous," instead of, "You know what, maybe?" —they are not going to be able to tolerate them as a couple. And there is no reason in the world that you shouldn't expect to be with someone who is both willing and able to validate your experiences. "But understand that it can be hard for someone who hasn't been exposed to racism, someone who may have even perpetuated it at times in their own lives. That's really a big challenge," says Orbe-Austin, "but that's something you need to be looking out for in the relationship, because racialized incidences do happen and *will* happen, most likely, if you live anywhere in America, and it's going to happen at least once over the course of the relationship and you have to have the resources as a couple to deal with it."

When Swirls Collide

First of all, wanting to be understood doesn't make you a needy, overly sensitive card-carrying member of the NAACP, nor should it scare him off. "You want to own your own feelings, and make sure that the discussion is personal, not accusatory," says psychotherapist and relationship expert Joyce Morely of Atlanta. "You can simply begin by saying: I believe we're getting closer, but I'm a little concerned. I'm afraid. I've heard some things about dating, say, an Asian guy, and I'd like to share them with you and I'd like for you to be honest with me about what you're thinking, and you open up the discussion right there."

As for your rainbeau man, it's important that you give him the exact same cultural consideration, only in a different sort of way. "When you're dealing with an ethnic man, you're dealing with an intergenerational conflict between a traditional upbringing and a more Western liberal environment, so these are men who grew up in a collectivist culture that prides itself on being very close knit with their family and their relatives," says Faizal Sahukhan, PhD, author of *Dating the Ethnic Man, Strategies for Success* in an interview with Christelyn on the *Beyond Black & White* blog. "The parents of these ethnic men fear a loss of their culture if their son dates someone outside of their ethnicity, a loss of their language and a loss of their religion, and these are key things that are integral in forming their ethnic identity."

> The one thing you need to do is educate yourself about his culture.

Get the feeling he's hiding you from the people he's closest to? It may not necessarily mean it's because he's ashamed of you, so don't go giving him the, "It's either me or your family" ultimatums too soon. "If you're really interested in fostering a nurturing relationship with your ethnic man," Dr. Sahukhan says, "do things to be accepted by his culture and by the people of his culture. The one thing you need to do is educate yourself about his culture. Ask your partner, or take courses, and learn about the culture and the things in the culture like the cuisine he's grown up with, his favorite foods. Learn about the religions and traditions, the fashion, the language. You don't have to conform yourself to these entities, but by having an understanding of these types of things you're validating his background, he feels appreciated, and he is then more prone to introducing you to his parents. If you have done all this and he tries to skirt the issue, then there are other things that need to be addressed. Those should be red flags that this guy could be a player or that he's not seeking a real relationship with you."

Share the Same Language

Now, open up and start talking. Communication is a key factor in any relationship, especially in one that is multiracial, multi-ethnics or mixed faith, and sometimes couples counseling can be necessary to help get the two of you really listening to what the other person is saying. "The secret X ingredient to any sustaining relationship is that both people are capable of being happy," says Seattle psychologist David Knopes, PhD. "You cannot have a loving relationship with a person who is always depressed or uncertain or incapable of receiving love; it's not just an emptying cup but that they're able to receive it, and in that way the people in the relationship are jockeying to provide that affection, that closeness, that intimacy, they're being sustained by their partner's efforts."

Taking a page from Dr. Gary Chapman's *New York Times* bestseller, *The 5 Love Languages,* Knopes says there are ways to keep you and your rainbeau continuing on your road to Happinessland. Just make sure to heed these road signs along the way:

Speak Love. There are times when words speak louder than actions, and affirming, unsolicited compliments can mean the world to you, and to your partner. Share words of kindness often and watch your relationship open up and soar to new heights.

Give Tokens of Affection. "Thinking of you" gifts don't have to be elaborate or expensive. A thoughtful gesture is priceless: It shows that you are cared for and you are valued.

Engage in Random Acts of Service. Washing the windows and cleaning the floors can speak volumes to show someone you care. Remember that the phrase "Let me do that for you" are the sweetest six little words anyone would love to hear.

Be a Soft Touch. Physical touch does not have to be sexual. A hug, holding hands, or even a thoughtful touch on the arm, shoulder, or face express excitement, concern, care, and love.

Spend Quality Time. Nothing shows your partner that you care more than your full undivided attention. Being there is critical, but really being there—with the TV off, fork and knife down, and all chores and tasks on standby—makes your significant other feel truly special and loved, and it keeps the relationship moving steadily along toward the next phase.

CHAPTER TWELVE

Janice

Let's Talk About Sex...
and Stereotypes

Penelope* was twenty-eight years old and in the middle of a nasty divorce in Texas when she met Thomas, a thirty-three-year-old security guard at her job, where she worked as an IT analyst. He was biracial—his father was Hispanic and mother was white—and, by her account, had been blessed with the beautiful blending of both: tanned skin, dark hair, and blue eyes. "I never thought that I would have been attracted to man who wasn't black—he had me smitten from his very first 'Hello,'" she recalls. As the weeks progressed, Penelope realized the relationship was becoming more intimate. "I, of course, had heard all the myths growing up about how white men have smaller penises and that they are terrible in bed, so needless to say I avoided the physical part of our relationship for as long as I possibly could," she says. "But the time came that it could not be avoided any longer and

I thought I'd just get it over with and 'fake it till he makes it.' Was I ever wrong! Not only was he well-endowed, it was as if I had experienced sex for the first time."

This now thirty-two-year-old nursing student's story isn't so uncommon. And I have run out of fingers and toes to count the number of times I have heard this long-held precept from black women that white men, and Asian men, are poorly endowed, terrible lovers, or otherwise unable to satisfy, egregious stereotypes that keep too many of us from exploring sexual encounters beyond black men. "It was a true adventure with Thomas," she says. "Up until that point, I always had to help myself along in reaching a climax. Not with Thomas. He always made sure that I enjoyed the experience as much as he did. I don't know if maybe it was youth or inexperience or if my ex-husband, who was black, was just selfish in bed, but with Thomas there was so much passion. He taught me what lovemaking truly feels like."

We think we have evolved into new-millennium modern-day thinkers, but black women all over the country, regardless of education and socioeconomic status, are living with age-old ideas when it comes to our consideration of the ideal sexual partner. We yearn to embrace our sexual bliss, and yet have allowed what our mothers, grandmothers, aunties, and sisterfriends have said about "them" keep us from pursuing something new. We know how hard it is to fight against the stereotypes of black women as lascivious, innately promiscuous, and even predatory, deviants—and yet we feel more than justified in projecting our own labels on others, unfairly sizing up men and defining their capabilities between the sheets (or lack thereof) based on what so-and-so-said instead of considering the realities of the individual that just might be the guy who can makes your toes curl.

The first time with any new partner can be wrought with the uncertainty of the unknown: Will he have enough going on down there to make it worth my while? And if he does, will he know how to use his equipment? Does he have "funky spunk"? Will he be a passionate lover, or just leave me all hot (and pissed off) after a quickie wham-bam? (Been there. Done that; but I should have known . . . he was a lousy kisser.)

Sex in a swirl, on the other hand, can conjure up questions of a more sorted sort: Can he measure up to the black men I've been familiar with? Will he want oral sex? Does he want to be with me, or does he just want to boink a black girl? Will he want shower sex? (And I just got my hair done!) Is this jungle fever? (If it is, then sex is likely the only thing on his mind, or in his conversation, and you should get rid of that one quick.)

Any guy who pressures you into doing something you really don't want to do is a first-rate ass, and by all means let him know it.

There's a general rule of thumb that applies to most sexual engagement: Any guy who pressures you into doing something you really don't want to do is a first-rate ass, and by all means let him know it. But lasting relationships are based on compromise—and lots and lots of it. And yet instead of considering reasonable alternatives that could heighten your sexual exploration—taking a bath together versus the shower, for example, or agreeing on a hand job instead of putting your mouth "down there"—too many of us allow fears to put the kibosh on our intimate adventures with men of other races or cultures. We decide instead to wallow in the familiarity of our comfort zones—even if that means the sheets on the other side of the bed are always cold.

Time to Get Real

Our thirty-six year old New York accounting assistant and single mom, Onica Cupido, never had any reservations about dating beyond black having been born in the West Indies, where racial and ethnic swirls abound between the islands populace of Indians, Asians, whites, Hispanics, and blacks. Although she came to America at the age of six, the makeup of men in Brooklyn, she says, was just about the same as it was back home, and her parents never balked when she brought home guys who were "different." It was, very simply, normal.

Twice married, her first husband was West Indian, her second Chinese, and she had heard the talk about Asian men lacking the suitable prowess to satisfy. "I never had an issue with size, or anything like that," she says. "I mean, size is impractical." But before she became proficient on the subject, she confesses that she was not without questions when it came to Asian men and sex. "But my curiosities were about sexual practices with some Asian men: How sexual are they? We don't see them in movies as being sexual beings, right? So when I started dating them, I'm wondering what happens when the lights go off?" So she decided to do some homework. "I asked my Asian girlfriends:

'Okay, what do Asian men do?'" she laughs, the idea of it now striking her as kind of funny. "But I was like: 'Are they going to be scared if I do this, or am I suppose to be shy, somewhat aggressive?'" Then, when she felt things were turning intimate with the man, she had a conversation with him. "I was like, 'Okay, what do you think sex with a black woman is like? I'm kind of curious about what things an Asian man will do or won't do.' Once you have that conversation you realize, like anything else, some people will do things that some other people don't do. Just go with it from there, and you know. It's all about the flow of information, and the information isn't flowing right."

Adds dating expert Deborrah Cooper: "To think that a man is better than any other based solely on his skin color is an insult to those men," says Cooper, author of *Sucka Free Love: How to Avoid Dating The Dumb, The Deceitful, The Dastardly, The Dysfunctional & The Deranged!* "There are Black men who are some true pipe layers, and plenty of White men that know how to flip it, smack it, and rub it down, too! The stereotype that Black men are packing the most below the waist is also a falsehood. Men of all races have Mr. Stubbies, average-sized penises and porn-star-worthy schlongs. Each of us deserves to be loved for the person that we are, not used to fulfill someone's fantasies."

In short—no pun intended, *really!*—it all comes down to the person, not his package—or the one he's wrapped in. So if you've decided to expand your horizons and start dating out, it's important that you also unload all of that plantation baggage. It's just too much for you and your potential rainbeau to carry. And stereotypes and misinformation about performance won't do anybody any good. Once you free your mind and open your heart, your body will follow.

If Curiosity Killed the Cat . . . What Could It Do to You?

Most certainly, a lot of what happens between a man and a woman sexually is based on curiosity says Joyce Morely, a psychotherapist and relationship expert in Atlanta. But, treading into a sexual relationship too soon, or with apprehensions, can lead you into emotional danger. "With women, when it comes to sex, there's an emotional tie," says Morely. "So the woman who was initially afraid to have sex with the white guy, then finds out later that it was great, what is she going to do with the emotions after that? In any relationship, you need to ask yourself: What do you want out of this relationship? What are you looking for? What do you want to get out of this? And if you know, then what happens after that?"

So you really need to take some time to deal with you, or you could be setting yourself up for emotional bankruptcy. "A man can have sex with anybody," says Morely. "And he can have sex with you in the morning and then someone in the afternoon and another person at night. When it comes down to it, he's looking for something special, and that may be in one of us or none of us. When a man sleeps with a woman, he may not want anything from her tomorrow. With women, we want something tomorrow. We want something that's mine. Men don't emotionally invest. They know that it's just sex. Women don't know how."

But, she says, be mindful: jumping into bed to quell your

curiosities or hoping to satiate your partner is wrought with its own issues. "When you invest your body, are you investing your mind into it? Are you investing emotionally? What's the investment, and what are you looking for in terms of a pay-off?" Morely offers, "Make sure you're investing the part that you might be willing to lose. It's just like the stock market. If you're not in it for short-term losses, then don't invest in the stock market. Same goes for women. Don't be investing in it if you're not ready to take the loss." That Penelope, our white man convert, had her fears about sex with white men assuaged, later opening her up to other intimate relationships with non-black men, hitting the sheets and hoping it will be okay denies you—and your partner—the opportunity for some honest dialogue and true intimacy, and it could ultimately doom the relationship before it has a chance to be good. "A lot of what this woman might not be telling you is not just that she wanted to 'get it over with,' but her own fear of "What if this man is going to reject me because *he* doesn't see me as beautiful anyhow?" Dr. Morely says. "It's a self-fulfilling prophecy. You can't have this relationship. It's almost like: I'm not going to set myself up for failure. I'm not going to set myself up to be rejected. So I'll go ahead and sabotage it myself so no one else can throw me out with the trash. I'll throw myself out."

It has to do with how we, ourselves, have been stereotyped throughout generations, "which plays a lot of into our psyche," Morely continues, "because we, as African American women, don't see ourselves as beautiful. So there are women who don't expect anyone else to see them as beautiful. It's their own lack of esteem, and no one really wants to talk about it, but it goes back to the plantation. It's part of the fiber of this country."

It is further reinforced in our pop culture. Sure, *Basketball Wives* and *The Real Housewives of Atlanta* are some of our favorite guilty pleasures, but to think that media images of ourselves does not have an impact on how we see ourselves sexually, or on how others—especially rainbeau men—see us, is not only wrongheaded, but naive. Just think about the images you see of black women in movies and on television. How often do you see successful, three-dimensional, loving black women with healthy, unencumbered sexual appetites whom men find romantically alluring and engaging? If you can name more than a handful over the past decade, then you're doing better than most of us that follow entertainment media for a living. Having devoted much of my twenty-year journalism career to media and pop culture, I can say most assuredly that when it comes to black women and sexuality, the picture—be it on the big or little screen—is not a pretty one.

Don't Believe the Hype: Your Black Is Beautiful

For the most part it is rare to see our images on screen anywhere, and when we exist in scripted narratives at all, it is most very often in one-dimensional roles where a black woman have little semblance of a life outside her interactions with her more predominant, usually white counterparts who get to have all the well-rounded exploration of their lives—including their love lives.

On the big screen, where black women and sex is involved, it's the asexual, nurturing mammy who takes care of white people and their children—and this has been going on for generations from Hattie McDaniel's Academy Award–winning turn in the 1939 classic _Gone with the Wind,_ to one of the most hyped films of 2011, _The Help,_ starring Tony winner and Academy Award nominee Viola Davis. Over the years, not much has changed in how the mammy is portrayed—not only does she not have time to prioritize herself or her own family, and most certainly not her sex life, the role is typically cast as a larger, darker, older woman who is generally desexualized on camera.

If you don't have the mammy, you again have ages-old Jezebel and Sapphire stereotypes where the woman is a loose, slutty bad girl who is a bad influence on everybody around her, who is out to get men into trouble, someone who is intentionally poking holes in condoms so that she can be a babymama and so she can get money out of the guy. Black filmmakers themselves are not immune to falling into these stereotypes of black women. In _She's Gotta Have It,_ Spike Lee's debut lauded for its provocative portrayal of a black women's sexual independence, is marred by the brutal scene in which protagonist Nola Darling is raped as a result of her sexual openness, falling into the all too familiar tropes about black women's sexuality and about how a black woman who enjoys sex, who talks about what she wants and goes after what she wants, has to be punished. More recently, Tyler Perry also fell into similar stereotypes with his adaptation of _For Colored Girls,_ in which Ntozake Shange's visceral Tony-nominated play featuring seven women's stories representing the specific individual challenges facing black women, even as the group presents the community's collective experience, "devolved into soap opera of victimized women endlessly tormented at the hands of a slurry of black men, sick cartoons, existing only to perpetuate horrors on the women," wrote *The Hollywood Reporter*'s Kirk Honeycutt in his review of the film.

"That's why *Waiting to Exhale* was so unusual when it came out," says Jennifer L. Pozner, founder and director of Women in Media & News in New York, "because it had black women having sex lives and not being ashamed about it, and being full people. Now the film had its limitations, but at the very least these women didn't feel like they had to apologize for wanting relationships and wanting sex, and the men in that movie found them attractive whether they were skinny or heavy, younger or older, there were just a wide variety of women who were allowed to access the human experience of relationships."

Pozner, also the author of *Reality Bites Back: The Troubling Truth About Guilty Pleasure TV,* which offers a blistering examination of how the reality TV genre has turned back the societal clock thirty-five years by perpetuating outdated gender myths, racial stereotypes, and backwards ideals of sexuality and body image that are in no way reflective of our modern society. It's easy for us to chalk it up to the mindless TV fluff that assuages our own realities at the end of a long day, but there are serious social implications that need to be addressed. Since this book is all about dating and mating, let's look at broadcast TV reality dating shows. First of all, there are hardly any, if ever, black women (or any women of color, for that matter) among the twenty-five ladies vying for the affections of the white hunkaliciousness on shows like ABC's *The Bachelor*. Whereas when you look at cable, dating shows like *Flavor of Love, For the Love of Ray J,* and *I Love New York,* showcase black women as hypersexual promiscuous gold diggers who are loud, mean, ignorant, and mercenary—not exactly the kind of fun, smart, sensual, caring, loving women with whom a man would want to have any real relationship.

Let's take it a step further with scripted shows. Even when you have a powerful, intelligent, black woman in a scripted format, like Chandra Wilson's Dr. Miranda Bailey in ABC's popular television series, *Grey's Anatomy,* that ideal rarely translates sexually. Consider all the sex going on in the fictitious Seattle Grace Mercy West Hospital, and still we have yet to see no-nonsense Bailey in any kind of a sexual tryst either on or off the job, even though her romantic life has been explored, albeit marginally, in the series that is executive produced and written by an African American woman, Shonda Rhimes. It is a perplexing situation, to which Pozner poses: "Is a strong black woman having sex just too powerful or too scary for white audiences to handle? Or is it so inconceivable because there's never been a very good template for a good, fleshed-out black female character to be strong and also sexy that if you show Bailey having sex that all of a sudden her character is now devalued [as] the Jezebel? Who knows? Maybe it's all of that, but we just don't have enough templates."

With black women falling into roles as victims, sex workers, sidekicks, or the various shameful slut roles that further reinforce cultural sexual stereotypes, it's not a wonder then that when it comes to depictions of black women in interracial relationships, the pictures is decidedly skewed there as well, says Latoya Peterson, owner and editor of the multiracial site Racialicious.

"We focus a lot on pop culture," says Peterson, "because that's where a lot of people get their cues about society—like why do little girls grow up dreaming of their wedding day? Your mom might tell you one thing, but most women are looking at all the bridal shows, the pomp and circumstance, the happy endings in your favorite movies and the fairytales manufactured by Disney, all that stuff results in marriage. So when little girls dream of being a bride or being a princess, this is all the extensions of that same fantasy.

"What we notice about interracial relationships in pop culture," Peterson continues, "is presented in one of two ways. The first is racial conflict at the core of your relationship. You can see this in *Sex and the City*. There were very few people of color on *Sex and the City*, in general, but when they were on screen there was always this weird kind of adversarial relationship, and in one instance it was centered on Miranda's storyline with Blair Underwood playing her love interest, but more so with Samantha, when she was sleeping with a black man. Her encounters were completely adversarial particularly with black women, and [in one scene] they surround her and say, Why you takin' our man? What's wrong with you? And she comes back with very defiant attitude, 'I will wear whatever and blow whomever I want as long as I can breathe and kneel,' and that's her flippant remark and she walks away. But there is never a conversation about why black women really feel that way or what cultural dynamics are at play there, it's just strictly adversarial relationship where people in interracial relationships are shown to be the objects of confrontation, the objects of harassment, which puts out that sort of subtle message that you don't want to mess with this because there's going to be so much drama, it's easier and safer to stick with your own kind, and that's a really damaging message to get, but that's the message that's being sent when mixed race couples are always the recipient of adversarial action."

On the flip side of that, "you have the Shonda Rhymes universe, which is super multiracial, in terms of people mixing," says Peterson, "but there's never any kind of conversation about why that's happening. That's also equally problematic, and it's not that we don't want to see these relationships where it revolves around more than just people and their races, but at the same time, race is a big part of our lives, and there's a big fear for a lot of people that are dating interracially that their partner will say or do something that is racist toward them or racist toward members of their group and they don't know how to handle that.

"One of the hardest things to moderate on a multiracial website are dating posts, because they're so fraught with racial misunderstanding and people's own internalized stereotypes and their own hate about maybe themselves, with the projections they put upon other people, with ideas of racial solidarity," Peterson notes. "It's what my colleague, Carmen, calls 'voting with your pussy,' meaning you can't really be Asian American anymore if you're not dating a guy who's not Asian American, if you're not down with the cause, like there's all these ideas that are wrapped up into who we date and our identity. Which makes it easy for people to kind of fall back on the comfort of stereotypes."

In his NPR segment on the too-perfect world of television's interracial couples, Eric Deggans, *Tampa Bay Times* television and media critic, questions why series executive producers are unwilling, or unable, to address these issues realistically as they are in the real world. Among the growing number of shows that featured interethnic partnerships, he points to a few pairings from shows that were on the air during the 2010–11 television season, including Mike and Lisa (white man, Asian woman) on Fox's *Traffic Light;* Alice and Alonzo (white woman, black man) on ABC's *Mr. Sunshine;* and Jasmine and Crosby (black woman, white man) on NBC's *Parenthood,* who were so mismatched they couldn't even load the dishwasher together—and yet, when it came to their racial and cultural differences, they weren't even discussed. "On its face, this seems like tremendous progress. It's a world where interracial couples face no disappointed parents, no odd questions from neighbors, no total strangers asking why their kids are different colors," but for Deggans, who is black and has been married to a white woman for nearly twenty years, "a world where interracial couples almost never discuss race doesn't feel real. What it feels like is avoidance."

> A world where interracial couples almost never discuss race doesn't feel real. What it feels like is avoidance.

David Kronke, a freelance television journalist in Los Angeles, offered his thoughts on the situation. "Producers, first of all, want to appeal to as large of an audience as possible," says Kronke, affectionately known around these parts as the Mayor of Television, who is a frequent contributor to the *Los Angeles Times, TV Guide,* and the industry trade daily, *Variety.* "But more often than not," he continued, "producers are trying to make a statement by introducing such a dynamic, even if that statement is merely, 'We're not commenting on race because we don't think it's a big deal and you shouldn't either.'"

Ah, now if only Hollywood could market the rose-colored shades to the rest of America.

Don't be fooled, says Pozner. In the end, "nothing—not creative quality, not social impact, and certainly not accountability to the public—matters to media companies other than the financial bottom line." A stern reminder of why it is even more important that we scrutinize our own media for what it continues to perpetuate about us.

Our Bodies, Our Images, Our Selves

As opportunities begin opening up for more African American women to create images and tell stories of a more diverse black female experience, we can flip the script in our own lives, too, says Young. "We need to begin encouraging ourselves, and quite specifically encouraging our daughters, to really interrogate and engage the media they're watching and be absolutely critical. The way we talk about ourselves, the way we treat ourselves and treat one another is important, too."

Not only that, we need to begin to do some swirling of sorts among our sisters of other cultures and hues, says Morely. "A lot of the attitudes about us have to do with how white women, and other women, see black women," she says. "Just the level of disrespect that is garnered among women is appalling. When women don't know how to accept and respect each other, then men begin look at that also in how they see black woman. So, number one, we need to begin having that conversation with other women.

"Number two," Morely continues: *"Black women have to start giving themselves permission to be beautiful.* They can't be given permission by someone else: Look at that mirror on the wall and what does that mirror say to you about you? And having that *mmm hmmm* time with yourself where you're actually accepting you for who you are and you're not being defined by someone else as important. You already know you're beautiful, you already know that you're sensual and sexy and sexual, and when that man comes along, when you've already validated that for yourself, it won't be hard for you to believe that someone sees it no matter what color he is."

Unless you're a supermodel, getting naked in front of a man for the first time can be less than ego boosting for any woman, according to Laure Redmond, author of *Feel Good Naked.* We all have hang-ups about our appearance, but allowing insecurities about body image can totally mess up what could be a pleasurable experience. So give yourself a mental makeover, and have that *mmm hmmm* time with yourself the next time you step out of the shower. Stand in front of a full-length mirror and take a look at yourself from head to toe—a really good look. Then start appreciating what you see. Go on, try it. I dare you. It can be wonderfully affirming. It is why I can smile and say hello to a man walking my way without wondering what *he* thinks of me—that's really none of my business, or my concern. That is why, when I'm with a man, I don't need to question why he wants to be with me as a black woman. And the same goes for me. It is the man I'm wanting, not his color, his culture, or his religion, albeit the lovely added accoutrements that rainbeaus can bring.

And any sex expert worth their salt will tell you that when you find a man who really wants to be with you, he isn't so concerned about those extra few pounds around your waist or the dimple in your left butt cheek—and neither should you. Close encounters outside your race don't have to be a foreign affair. So go ahead: put on that sexy lingerie, spray on some perfume— throw a little music on to get you in a playful or sexy mood, and go for it, girl.

PART III

When It Gets Really Serious

CHAPTER THIRTEEN

Christelyn

Love Is Blind... But Not Those People Staring at You!

I'll just come right out and say it. I used to be on high alert when my husband and I started dating.

Here's him: "Hey, babe, there's some good jazz at [insert urban venue with more chocolate than vanilla, strawberry, or lemon sherbet] and I thought, since you like it so much, we could go."

Then here's me: Pausing, processing the percentage of black people whose eye daggers I'd have to deflect and weighing it against how much I love jazz, I would say, *"Aww honey, can't we just make some dinner at home, read* Newsweek *and just listen to 94.7 The Wave?"*

If I could help it, I avoided going places where clusters of black people hung out. They stared, outright gawked with mouths so wide birds could build their starter homes in them.

Once Mike picked me up from a beauty salon in a predominantly African American side of town to take me to dinner. He walked in, cute and smiling, complimenting me, joking (like always) that it smelled like charred Barbie hair. The salon, which so happened to be the same spot Shaquille O'Neal got his head shaved, was abuzz with the usual gossip, cackling laughter, and hip hop songs. But all the noise came to a screeching halt when he walked in—you know, kind of like that dream you have when you show up for school without your pants.

Can't say I wasn't a little uncomfortable with the hairy eyeball, but *not* uncomfortable enough to drop this cutie. He took me to the Philharmonic and museum and on mini weekend trips to Catalina Island and introduced me to his United Colors of Benetton group of friends, two of whom would be in our bridal party. He was the nicest, funniest, most considerate man I had ever met. No way was I dropping him.

So I picked places that were more racially diverse to hang out—it was affirming to see other couples that looked like us. Problem (mostly) solved.

You'll Have to Make a Few Adjustments

Although things are changing, being in an interracial relationship can sometimes be uncomfortable for both you and your rainbeau. This may be your first time stepping out of your comfort zone, and you must also consider that this is a first for him, too. Be open about it, acknowledge it, but don't dwell on it. Focus, focus, focus on the guy, on his character and whether or not he makes you happy and would be a good life partner and father to your future children. Don't be so concerned with what other people might be thinking. What matters most is what you and your guy think of *each other.*

Let me give it to you straight: Grow some skin. The thick kind. If your rainbeau is The One, that skin will come in handy. After being with my husband for more than a decade and four kids later, I couldn't care less who stares. To grow thick skin takes time. I came to realize that I was with a wonderful man, who loved me deeply, took care of me, thought I was beautiful, and loved my first daughter as if she were his own. Were those people staring at me, supporting, and adoring me? At some point, I had to stop worrying about what other people thought of my interracial relationship and focus on what really mattered: My happiness. So should you.

> I had to stop worrying about what other people thought of my interracial relationship and focus on what really mattered: my happiness.

It Comes with the Territory

Unless you are being eyeballed because you have grown a Smurf on your forehead, face the fact that some people will do a double take when you're out with your rainbeau. How many bugged-out eyeballs and gaped mouths you encounter will largely depend on the progressiveness of your city or town and which region of the country you reside.

Kenya, twenty-eight, a Yale graduate and a successful lobby-ist in Washington, D.C., recently began her first-ever interracial relationship with a white guy she met online. Things were get-ting pretty serious (the "l" word had been thrown around); how-ever, Kenya felt self-conscious and angry when others stared at her when she was out with him, so much so that she had more than once considered ending the relationship. Her boyfriend was oblivious to the stares, which made it even more frustrat-ing because she felt like she couldn't really talk to him about her feelings.

The constant sense that you're under a microscope can add extra strain to an interracial relationship for sure. But accord-ing to Linda Young, PhD, a psychologist who specializes in in-terracial relationships in Seattle, Washington, how you manage those feelings depends on how you interpret the situation. "The person on the receiving end of a stare can interpret it in a way that could hurt their feelings, or be neutral, or make them feel stronger. Depending on what's going on in that woman's brain when she sees the stare, she can walk away from it feeling pow-erful, good, terrific, indifferent, or upset." In other words, it's all in how you take it.

Staring is natural and not always done with malevolent in-tent. Kenya's annoyance might not *necessarily* mean that those people are bigots—they just might have been curious. "Our brains are naturally wired to go to what is novel and unique," says Patti Wood, a body language expert with a specialty in intercul-tural communication. It's part of the hunter/gatherer instinct, so you can blame your ancestors for this irksome behavior.

Why They Stare: They Want a Rainbeau, too!

Others may be looking at you because they want to *be* you. You can thank the media influences that beat us over the head about how desperately single we are. Or you can do what I think most black women are doing when considering dating out. They weigh the options and use their God-given common sense. So naturally, more women and nonblack men who are on the fence are taking notice.

Jacquie, a single black woman who frequents my blog, *Beyond Black & White*, told me this:

> *I am an interracial gawker! I was just thinking the other day like "dang, a lot of sistas are getting their swirl on ... with some very nice looking men!" I mean, ya'll just sort of stick out with the holding of the hands, or pulling out the seat of a chair, or feeding lil' Tiffany or Jason sooo affectionately—hehe LOL I feel like my grandmother used to look when watching old black & white movies: tears in the eye, sappy smile, and hands clutched to the chest!! I try not to stare, I really do, but when I get caught I think my face/expression is one of appreciation and support. Sometimes, I have to catch myself from just saying "Thank you for being an example" and keep it moving, but I wouldn't want that to come off in an offending manner, either.*

Masha, another reader, said straight up,

> *"I confess, I do it. Not because I am mad at her, but because I am deeply happy for the woman."*

And sweet, young Nadell:

I must admit, I am an interracial gawker in a way of admiration and to somehow get a kodak moment of that couple's love!! I'm single at the moment so seeing an interracial couple gives me a great deal of inspiration and motivation! I remember attending the theater for a jazz performance and this one couple had seats beside me or a couple of seats away . . . she was black and he was Asian and I mean the most eye-pleasing couple I ever did see! My gosh, they were just gorgeous together! He held her hand and she laid her head on his shoulder as the music played—I found myself making every effort to direct my eyes towards them in the most reserved, not so obvious way . . . it was crazy because I barely paid any attention to the performance because of my gawking!

In the more benign cases, there are strategies you can employ that could serve as an opportunity to teach, diffuse, or otherwise make the starer find something else bright and shiny to look at. When managing the stares of the curious or the furious, you basically have three choices: *acknowledge, ignore,* or *confront.*

ACKNOWLEDGE

Acknowledging the stares and curiosity of oglers doesn't even require you to open your mouth. It's all about body language and nonverbal signals that can put you and strangers more at ease with one another in a nonthreatening way. This technique will probably work optimally with more nonthreatening individuals, like the elderly, children, and other women. Wood suggests a head-tilt-smile combo:

- Woods suggests to look back, but do two things to show that you are comfortable and make them comfortable. Make eye contact, tilt your head slightly to the side, and smile. "The smiles says, 'I'm friendly and I'm happy.'" (Here's my tip—try this tactic in the mirror a couple times so you don't look like you're trying out for a beauty pageant.)

Blogger BlackGirlinMaine agrees that a smile usually does the trick. "It's been nineteen years since my first interracial relationship, and at this stage in life I stare back at folks. Depending on my mood, I may smile or if I sense they disapprove I hit 'em with the stank eye. To be honest I rarely do that, generally I find a direct stare back and a smile breaks the ice and we can move on."

- Don't slouch. On a primal level, our distant cousins in the primate family try to shrink and appear smaller and nonthreatening in the face of a formidable foe.

IGNORE

This is by far the safest and least stressful tactic; because let's not be naive: Some stares you encounter will be clearly meant to communicate disapproval. In this case, the offender is deliberately looking for your acknowledgment and attention. Don't feed the troll. Here's a few suggestions on how to handle these jackasses:

- Don't look for approval *or* disapproval. Try not to scan to room looking for people who might be giving off negative vibes. This makes you appear vulnerable and not confident in your choice. You send knuckle draggers the message and the courage to feel it's okay to meddle. Keep your eye on *your* prize.

Elle, who is in a serious relationship with a white rainbeau, has the right idea.

I know people stare and talk, but I am so in love with my man that everyone else literally fades into the background, white noise as far as I am concerned. I think it bothers my boyfriend more, so to make sure he is focusing on the right thing I make sure he gets my attention and I let him be affectionate in public because I know he gets insecure or unsure. I smile at him often, make eye contact, hold his hand securely . . . I even go as far as saying "I love you" loud enough for spectators to hear. It's not about making a show, but trying to ingrain in a stranger's mind that interracial couples are just as loving, "normal," carefree, and secure as same-race couples.

- Look *through* people, rather than *at* them. Locking eyes with them only gives rude starers encouragement to continue to be obnoxious.

Toni is a pro at a tactic I often use when one of my children hurls themselves to the floor, flopping and foaming at the mouth in a tantrum: I pretend I don't see it. "I'm pretty good at looking right through people—especially when I *know* they are staring. I perfected this technique long before I started dating out. I went to a predominantly white school as an undergrad in a very white, small Midwestern town where white people would stare at you for no other reason but for the fact that you are black. So I learned to look right through them. I'm no longer in that town (thank goodness!)—but when I'm out with my boyfriend—especially in majority black areas—I look right through the people I know are staring. I really don't care; most of them aren't happy anyway and are resentful of what you have," she says.

CONFRONT

This strategy is one I least recommend—except with children. Kids are a tabula rasa, and their minds are still open and teachable. If the opportunity arises at, say, the grocery store, and some five-year-old points and says, "Look, Mommy! That white guy is with a brown girl!" This is a great time to tell that little girl or boy that love comes in all colors, and you chose your mate because what's on the inside is more important than what's on the outside. "Mommy" might get the drift, too.

But if you're ballsy like my friend Eugenia, you can take that ego down a peg. "I've only confronted a couple of times that I remember and it was with some black men who decided they didn't approve of my relationship with my ex-husband. I said, 'If I wasn't with him, I wouldn't be with you!' That usually got my ex-husband and myself laughing at their shocked faces, I don't think they expected me to say something."

A Note About Safety

Fortunately things have changed dramatically since the radical 1960s, but just because Barack Obama was elected president doesn't mean everyone is ready to hold hands and sing "Kumbaya." On rare occasions, disapproval can be overt and downright dangerous.

Sometimes it's best to avoid situations where confrontations are more likely. After all, your health and well-being is more important than a few hurtful words. Angela, an eighteen-year-old high school senior, reached out to me on Facebook about a white boy she's been crushing on, and who she invited to her high school prom. They were already friends, so he didn't hesitate to say yes. She was gleeful at first, then reality set in—apparently her Boston high school had recently had some racially charged incidents. And, *gasp!* None of her family members had ever engaged in the swirl, and she worried about the reception her friend might get when she brought him home. "I did this on a whim, never actually considering some important factors that could ruin a perfectly awesome night," she told me.

Now Angela has some very valid concerns. If there have been race-fueled violence at her school in the past, then she may need to take some extra steps to ensure she and her date have a good time. I told her that the odds of the least amount of confrontation at the dance was to "play the middle," which in this case, means gravitate to tables and dance areas with the most diverse group. In her case, I didn't recommend she or her date confront anybody. Acknowledging your excitement and happiness to others or ignoring them altogether is best in this case.

Ready-to-Fight Body Language Signals

Rob Riggs, a personal security expert, veteran, and bodyguard, says that there are body language signals that aggressors use before they act. Look for these signals:

- Invasion of your personal space quickly.
- Aggressors may "fake you out" and pretend to attack to gauge your response.
- Don't lock eyes with a potential assaulter. Focus on the shoulders and the chest, because any attack will most likely initiate from that part of their body. "Look for a shoulder to cock, or a fist to double up," says Riggs.

But Rigg's best advice is to not be brave beyond your means. "If you think a person is going to be a threat, why would you want to stick around?" In most cases, the wisest (and safest) response to overt and potential aggressive disapproval is to just skedaddle.

If you find yourself cornered, like in Angela's case, let your purse be your protector. Some states may even allow stun guns. And if you live in Oklahoma, like Riggs, you can carry heat around like an extra accessory.

The last word: Don't be hamstrung by fear because it is bound to cripple your relationship and your psyche. Legitimate fear and concern for your safety is healthy. Being in a constant state of hyperalert is not. The odds are overwhelmingly in your favor that the wolves will howl from the cheap seats, so just keep it moving.

CHAPTER FOURTEEN

Christelyn

Dealing with Conflicting Loyalties

Lindsey's Story

Lindsey, a twenty-three-year-old African American girl, likes white boys. At three or four years old, her first crush was Jonathan Taylor Thomas, the blond-haired, blue-eyed son of Tim Allen's character from the hit 1990s show *Home Improvement*. Then her heart throbbed for Macaulay Culkin. "I didn't know what his name was, so I just called him Home Alone," she told me. She likes white guys with dark hair who are artsy and cultured, if not a bit nerdy.

Her proclivity toward white men seemed like the most natural thing in the world until she hit puberty, but thereafter something she couldn't quite put her finger on put the skids on her grand plans to be Mrs. Culkin. The source of that niggling feeling that was not okay to love someone who wasn't black came mostly from her fifty-one-year-old mother, who would rather her daughter find her IBM (ideal black man) or just be alone—like she has been since Lindsey was born and her father skipped out. "For my mother, it's black over everything. It makes me feel closed in and not able to make my own decisions. I feel like I have to hide myself."

Lindsey has not opted to expand her dating options because of any real or perceived shortage. She never had a desire to date black men. She had crushes here and there, but never anything serious. And for that she felt guilty. "I was embarrassed about it because I felt like you had to give black men a try first."

So what the cuss is wrong with her? In order to really understand what's going on with Claudia's mother, you have to be cognizant of what the world looked like when she was coming of age. Her mother was born right smack in the middle of the civil rights era and Jim Crow. Also television, which for the first time broadcasted the brutality against blacks and other civil rights supporters nationwide, in real time. Perhaps Lindsey's mother's suspicion arose from seeing the march from Selma to Montgomery, Alabama, in 1965. Or perhaps she saw news of Vernon Dahmer, a black community leader, killed in a Klan bombing in Hattiesburg, Mississippi. And probably what sealed her distrust for certain, when the world watched in horror as Walter Cronkite announced that Dr. Martin Luther King Jr. was assassinated in Memphis on April 4, 1968.

"White men got their bad reputations the hard way—they earned it," says author Roslyn Holcomb, who was born and raised in Alabama. Roslyn, forty-six, grew up during Claudia's mother's generation, and she knows firsthand what black women had to go through with white men "taking liberties" with them because they felt entitled to do so. Her mother, who worked as a maid for a white family, was once forcibly accosted by the white husband. The wife walked in during the assault, and laid square blame on Roslyn's mother for "seducing" the man, and was then subsequently fired. At Christmas.

With all that sordid history, one can understand why black women who grew up in the thick of things feel like dating and mating with a white man is like a betrayal—like sleeping with the enemy. And then, there was the Black Power movement in the 1970s, when finally black women adamantly rejected the advances of white men who only sought them out as objects of their fantasies and sexual desires. So Claudia's mother's disapproval of interracial intermixing is understandable, but it's 100 percent unfair of her to project it upon her daughter who says, "I don't think that just because you share the same skin color means you can only be attracted to them."

Is it a generational thing? Perhaps. Writer Katty Gray, fifty, has never been married and loves black men because she feels they are the only male species on the face of the Earth that can understand what it is truly like for a black woman living in America. "There are preference for many reasons. I like the aesthetic, I like how black men look, I like music and the culture." Katty is a beautiful dark-brown skinned woman, with full lips, hips, and a fabulous smile, and keeps her head shaved almost bald. She has been approached by nonblack men, sure. But she feels like their interest is more fetish than attraction and has rebuffed any overtures from nonblack men. Never having been married and facing the very real possibility that she may enter her senior years alone, she has a natural desire to find a mate. "It's unnatural to be alone. But I've always had that desire." But with a white boy? Not on her life.

"The first men I loved were the men in my family. My father, my brothers, my uncles, my cousins, and the boys on my block that let me build hot rods with them. I never imagined in my wildest dreams that I would be fifty and single, and I don't blame that on black men, and I've had my share of them. I think the fact the black people have not done a better job of mating black-to-black is a whole other commentary."

David's Story

David, twenty-six, is Hmong, part of an ancient ethnic group from the mountains of China. He's Asian, but he has the Barry White–smooth voice tailor-made for radio after dark. And like the dearly departed Barry, he loves black women. But that has caused some concern within his family. As an ever shrinking population of Hmongs, David's family wants him to settle with a nice Chinese girl and have pretty little Chinese babies. So when he married a black woman twice his age with two kids, the Vang family went into a tizzy—they thought David was having some kind of nervous breakdown.

David's choice in women is a huge deal, because the Asian culture is traditionally quite communal. The family is every-thing, and many men will not go against their families to be with another minority—especially African American. I heard one horror story about a black woman who tolerated her role as a mistress to the Asian man she loved, while he brought the family-approved stand-in home for the holidays. Some Asian men face tremendous pressure to comply with the family's wishes, or face estrangement or outright disinheritance. But just as all blacks from the African diaspora are not monolithic, the same holds true for Asians. In truth, some East Asian nationalities are more amenable and accepting of interracial relationships—namely Filipinos, Hawaiians, Cambodians, and Samoans (based on interviews). And with some other groups—Koreans namely—it can be a really, really tough sell to some families.

David has since been divorced from the older woman, but his yen for black women has not waned. Much to the chagrin of his family, he's currently seeing another chocolate woman closer to his age, and it looks to be a pretty serious affair. But as far as David's family accepting Chibi, eighteen, with open arms, things don't look good. "I *know* that my immediate family is not accepting of her. I've spoken to them about her but they refuse to meet her," David continues. "Whether I want them to meet her or not, they've made it clear that they don't want to meet her or get to know her. Due to that fact, I choose not to bring her and make her uncomfortable in any way. The last thing I want to do is put her in a situation where she has to feel like she has to be attacked verbally."

It's for that kind of resistance, any woman dating a rainbeau could face disapproval and rejection from the family of the man she loves. Diane Farr, actress and author of *Kissing Outside the Lines: A True Story of Love and Race and Happily Ever After*, wrote of the shock she felt when her then boyfriend, now husband, told her that his family might not be happy about their union, because she was white. She writes that her husband, Seung (whom she dubbed "The Giant Korean") was told by his parents from childhood that he was supposed to marry a Korean girl. "It didn't matter what all this meant because I could now see Seung was willing to fight for me. And that he was being torn in half by the idea of hurting me or hurting his parents," says Farr.

Both David and Claudia will have to make the decision—and take the risk—of being torn between the loves of their lives and the love of their families. As of late, Claudia has resolved to embrace her preference, but she still won't tell her mother. "I'll let my Facebook status tell her."

David has also has made his position clear. "I have addressed [remarriage] and they indicated that they would only [attend a wedding of mine] if they approved of the relationship. I told them that they should not hold their breath because [a wedding] *will* happen. I've told them that they are welcome only if they are coming to support us out of love and not losing face. As far as kids goes, that they can only see the child if they are able to come around because when they look at the child, they'll see me and her."

Swirling, Culture, and Family

Western culture is individualistic. We revel in the idea that we can go our own way, forge our own paths, make our own fortunes. We romanticize this notion in movies, books, folklore, and music. Beware, Western culture can easily clash with an Eastern, an African, or Hispanic one. Let's look at the cultures of Japan, China, Korea, most Arab countries, Mexico, Puerto Rico, Kenya, and Chile, for instance. You'll find, to a large degree, that they thrive on family, group, and/or tribal cohesiveness. The sons within these cultures have an incredible responsibility (and burden) to follow the wishes of their families or face not only rejection, but outright ostracism and risk completely being disinherited. Dating and marrying someone outside your race, tribe, or religion becomes a huge deal.

The book _Dating the Ethnic Man,_ by intercultural psychologist, Faizal Sahukhan, PhD, identifies the traits of a rainbeau from collective culture:

- He thinks in terms of collective gratification—"we" versus "I."
- He values the well-being of his family, his culture, and his society over his own personal well-being.
- He conforms to a groupthink mentality, sacrificing his individual thoughts, feelings, and actions in order to be part of the group.
- He cooperates with others in the group for group unity and cohesion, believes in maintaining a close relationship with his family of origin, even after marriage.

And here's the biggie:

- He considers it shameful to deviate from family and cultural expectations, and
- considers individualistic tendencies to be inappropriate and unhealthy.

It's those last two reasons that American women need to exercise a little more caution with dating ethnic men. I once briefly dated a Persian man whose family was from Iran. We were in the same literary class, and he and I were jockeying to be the smartest and most enlightened in the class. I outdid him over several debates on the interpretations of Edgar Allan Poe and Flannery O'Connor, and he was smitten. He began to sit right next to me in class and would follow behind me after it was over until he finally asked me out. I thought he had good potential—he was cute (but I could tell he'd be bald one day) and was on his way to medical school. What attracted him was my smarts, but when we were alone, it wasn't my brain he was after. In between pleas for me to sleep with him, I asked, "What would your parents do if they knew you were on a date with a black girl?" And then I pestered, "Would you ever marry a black girl?" He hemmed and hawed, but I never got a straight answer, and that guy never got into my pants. I wasn't going to catch feelings for that guy only to have them crushed when Mommy and Daddy threatened to disown him if he brought me home.

"It's really rare that an Iranian guy is going to marry you. If he does, consider yourself the exception to the rule. Is it right? No. But we're talking old-school generation here," says my best friend from college, Padideh Jafari (I call her PJ for short). She says it's a real cultural taboo to marry anyone, *anyone* who is not Middle Eastern. "They don't condone it. You could be exiled from the family."

When I first met PJ's parents, who emigrated from Iran after the fall of the shah in the 1970s—they thought I was African, because to them, Americans were always white. The only black people they knew while they lived in Iran were servants. They had no Westernized view at all. Black = African. First- and second-generation Iranians obviously understand blacks aren't slaves but the taboo still remains. Blacks are seen as a lower class, but for me, I was the exception. I was educated, well-spoken, and respectful of my elders. How could that be? After all, that's not what they saw on television. More often than not, foreign-born people glean their impressions of other this way, and then all black men are like 50 Cent and all black women are like NeNe Leakes. When I gave birth to my son, Zachary, Padideh and her mother, Zeba, came to visit in the hospital and see the baby. The first thing Zeba said (in Farsi, translated by PJ) was, "Oh! Your in-laws will be so happy because he is so white! What a blessing." PJ was mortified and embarrassed for me, yet,

> You can't force your ethnic rainbeau to bring you home and throw you at his parents and grandparents on the third date, or even the twentieth.

we looked at each other and silently understood. His expression of empathy proves that with each generation colorism and seemingly benign bigotry—becomes a little more watered down. Hopefully, it will wash away.

Bottom line: You can't force your ethnic rainbeau to bring you home and throw you at his parents and grandparents on the third date, or even the twentieth. If the man depends on the approval of his family, then things might turn out no bueno. One young lady who frequents my blog said, "I love Asian guys (I am currently in Asia) but I had a very bad experience dating one. Basically I met some of his family members (brothers) and after that, well, let's just say the relationship was doomed. I think someone said something about the fact that he was dating a black girl and he broke it off. It really broke my heart, he was my first love."

Ironically, as China expands their interests in other countries a growing number of Chinese men are marrying African women as the country spreads its chopsticks to Mother Africa. If you look deeper, this makes sense. There are quite a few cultural similarities. African women understand how marriage involves embracing the whole family and caring for and living with the in-laws once these elders are unable to live independently. There'll be no nursing home for Grandma, and African women have a firm understanding of these close family bonds.

One particular commenter on *Beyond Black & White*, a Chinese man with an MD and studying for his PhD, provided a list and it's so specific and hilarious I couldn't bear to parse the quote:

> *The dream woman needs to be an established professional, preferably in Health Care or Business or Academia and lawyers need not apply. On to the Great American Topic of Race in descending order. East Asian [Chinese, Korean, Southeast Asian, Japanese], South Asian [Indian, Pakistani, Bangladeshi, and Sri Lankan] with the qualifier of Rule Number One, partly because I like South Asians and also they get the whole multigenerational family values thing and can see why Grand-*

mother Chu is part of the package deal. We like the food and we both like Bollywood movies, even though we don't always understand the dialogue. Next are African descent women and bluntly, the darker the better. Everybody seems to have some sort of food comparison [Latte, Mocha, Milk chocolate, etc.] but I like more of a clarinet or oboe coloration myself. That's also negotiable, to a certain extent. Coming up at the end of the list are Latinas. That's the list, the whole list and nothing but the list.

The consensus is that when an Eastern man brings home a girl, it is to present the woman as a prospective wife for the approval of the family. So it's honestly a gamble. Rule of thumb, give your ethnic rainbeau a year, max. Don't waste your youth and precious reproductive years on someone who wants to hide you in the closet for half a decade.

Mamie Mooney, twenty-six, and her boyfriend, Tony, twenty-three, are struggling with how to introduce Mamie to Tony's Vietnamese parents. They're both in college, but unlike Mamie, Tony is completely dependent on the financial support of his family and must be considerate of their wishes until he graduates. As far as Tony's parents' know, he's not dating at all, because it is their expressed wish that he not date anyone until he graduates from college when he turns twenty-five. Add one more monkey wrench in the wheel—Mamie is divorced and has a two-year-old child. "He says that they don't mind the race of the person he is with a long as she is educated." (More on the meritocracy of swirling further down.) "But my biggest fear is that they won't accept me because I have a daughter. I feel like they will box me into that stereotypical black mother category and not approve of me for their son, and we plan to get married, but according to his culture, he has to ask them for permission." And like Diane Farr, the thought of Tony separating himself from his family wracks her with guilt, because she knows in the end he will choose her, because they are hopelessly in love. "Tony is the most amazing man I've ever met. The first time we met face-to-face I was in love. He was amazing with my daughter and we all played basketball and swords with sticks and tag. I can't imagine my life without him."

When it comes to dating an ethnic, particularly an Eastern man, Tony is probably the poster child. He's what social scientist called acculturative stress. According to psychologist John Berry, this state emerges when the traditional culture and new culture clash. These individuals "value and wish to maintain their cultural identity" while simultaneously "valuing and seeking out contact with those outside their own group and wish to participate in the daily life of the larger society," says Dr. Berry, who teaches and researches at Queen's University at Kingston in Ontario, Canada. The greater difference in original culture, the more pressure it is to assimilate into the dominant one.

The Eastern/Western Hybrid

We've covered the sweeping generalities of intercultural and multiethnic swirling, and we've also discussed the pressures by ethnic men to adhere to traditional norms. But there are exceptions, which are growing by leaps and bounds year by passing year. What happens when a first-, second-, or third-generation rainbeau merges Western traditions of individualism and Eastern values of communalism? You get a very confused guy who loves his family and background but will feel want to be a part of the bigger world (and people) around him.

Sometimes the choice is a bitter split altogether, like when Ricky Tsao, thirty-one, stopped speaking to his parents. Born in Shanghai, China, and immigrating to the United States at age seven, Ricky felt burdened by his mother and father's outrageous expectations of him—he has a master's in computer science from the University of Southern California—but his father was disappointed that he hadn't made the Ivy League. He tried to talk to his father about how all the pressure was taking a physical toll on his health. "I couldn't eat, I couldn't sleep. My father didn't believe me, and that hurt," says Ricky. After that, he told his parents he was going on a short trip to the East Coast, and just never came back. Now living in San Francisco with his African American girlfriend Danielle, twenty-six, of three years, he hasn't a worry in the world about whether or not his parents will accept their relationship, because he has not spoken to them since his "short trip." Ricky gives the ancient Chinese (by default) secret for screening whether or not an Eastern man is worth pursuing: "Ask him how close he is with his family. If he says they're everything to him (or something of that nature), that's a red flag for sure."

Denise Rodriguez, twenty-seven, an African American woman, was warned by her parents on the politics of color and encouraged her to marry a black man, because to marry "outside" could result in her future children being mistreated. So when they found out she was getting serious with Ernesto, a fourth-generation Mexican American, they hit the roof. Ernesto was completely assimilated, so much so that he didn't even speak Spanish, although most of his family could. Denise's father was surprisingly more upset that she was dating another minority and flat out told her that he'd rather see her married to a white man because together, they made a double minority couple. Her parents were so against their relationship that they skipped having a wedding and eloped. "They were shocked and so angry," she recalls. But funny how parents come around to the idea when children are involved. When she announced she was pregnant with their grandchild, now sixth months old, the motivation to have a relationship overruled any objections they might have had, and were even present at the hospital for the baby's birth.

Denise has heard of the "color" issue in the Mexican community and she says she "holds her breath" waiting for someone in her predominantly Hispanic neighborhood to say something. So far, so good.

Hispanic, Middle Eastern, Asian, and Indians have all been affected to some degree by colorism. Throw in India's caste system, where the light-skinned folks are at the top and the dark-skinned are at the very bottom, and where arranged marriages are customary, and things can become very, very complicated. Clara, an African American girl in her twenties who seriously dated an Indian man, told me, "We had some frank conversations about this topic and he acknowledged that he was 'okay' with dating me because I'm extremely fair. I asked if he would date me if I were darker and he admitted that he probably would not." The rise in skin bleaching products flying off the shelves seems to support what Clara's ex-boyfriend said. Fairer skin will get you better jobs and a chance to marry into a prominent family. But their skin-shade discrimination seems to be less focused on a legacy of European colonialism and more about whether your family worked hard in the fields or had cushy jobs made in the shade. "It indicates to someone who's meeting you for the first time that you are born into a family where you haven't had to do any outdoor work, and that your status is higher because you never had to be in the fields or do any of that," says Meenakshi Reddy Madhavan, who runs a blog called *The Compulsive Confessor*.

Sehnita Mattison, a native of Pakistan who was raised in Michigan, is a gorgeous South Asian woman who has skin the color of a penny. "Growing up, I always felt I wasn't good enough or pretty enough because I was darker than anyone else around me, including my parents," she says. She recalls how when after she'd come from a week away at band camp, several shades darker, her mom and dad noticed and "weren't too happy about it." She would go to the beach, she wore an all-over bodysuit instead of a bikini, not because she was being modest, but because she was concerned about getting too "baked." She does say that the color issue is not as rampant in the United States like it is in India, but it was enough for this beautiful, brown girl to feel less than beautiful.

Sehnita has been married interracially to a white guy for eleven years. For her family, an arranged marriage wasn't expected because more important than race was that her husband share the Christian faith. "I won't lie, I think my parents would have liked it if I found a nice Christian Indian guy!" So as an Indian, I felt like she would be a sound source about the prospects of interracial relationships with black women. She's frank about the color issue and admits that might be a potential snag. Acceptance into an Indian family increases if you have a fondness for the culture and the food. But she gives a warning: If an Indian man doesn't introduce you to his family once you're exclusive, be wary.

But Asians, like Hispanics and Middle Easterners, are not monolithic and cultural mores vary just as much as their skin shades do. In an informal study I discovered anecdotally certain races, like Filipinos, Hawaiians, Samoans, Cambodians and (increasingly) Chinese are more open to interracial mergers than others. And not all Latinos are hung up on hue. Iván López, a native of Spain, tells me that in his part of the country, skin shade is perceived a lot differently than in the United States.

"My parents, or any average Spaniard, don't distinguish between a 'full black,' a light skinned black, a mixed race black, a biracial, etc. All of them are 'people of color,' we could say." If there is any distinction, it is between Americans (whose status makes this equivalent to a WASP) and Africans. "I remember being a kid and watching *The Fresh Prince of Bel-Air* on TV with my granny, and she saying that [the] people were not black, they were café con leche [coffee with milk]. So, for her, the African

Americans she sees on television are not 'really black'. The authentic black people for her were the guys from Africa. Can you believe it?" As a matter of fact, Iván, yes I can.

As far as his preference for black women, Iván's family doesn't seem to mind. For them, it's like just having a preference, similar to how some men prefer blondes.

CHAPTER FIFTEEN

Christelyn

Handling the
Guess Who's Coming
to Dinner Moment

Unless you've been living under a rock in the mountain caves of Afghanistan, you've heard of the movie classic, *Guess Who's Coming To Dinner* starring Sidney Poitier, Spencer Tracy, and Katherine Hepburn. Poitier's character, John Prentice, meets his white fiancée's parents for the first time, and the fit hits the shan. For the younger crowd, you have likely seen *Guess Who?* the updated version where it's the white guy—starring that hunk of hotness Ashton Kutcher—comes to meet his black girlfriend's parents who aren't too keen on their daughter marrying a white boy.

When you get serious about your interracial or intercultural relationship you will likely have a *Guess Who?* moment. It might not be the parents. It could be Uncle Larry, former Black Panther, or cousin Bill, who has never met a black person. It could be Aunt Mae, who thinks all Chinese people own dry cleaners, and believes Mexicans speak . . . Mexican.

"While the couple may enjoy each other's differences, their families can be very uncomfortable with each other. Also, different regions of this country have different customs, so a southern family might feel quite foreign to a northeastern date. So, it's very important for the couple to talk about their family customs, traditions, and differences," says Tina B. Tessina, PhD (aka Dr. Romance), psychotherapist and author of *The Unofficial Guide to Dating Again*.

This event—the big unveiling of your rainbeau—can be a pivotal point in your relationship. How either one of you are received by family members can make an impact on how much all this is worth the trouble.

My *Guess Who?* moment with my husband was a disaster. In fact, the whole ordeal broke us up for a while. Mike flew me in from California to the foreign land of Westport, Connecticut, home of Michael Bolton, the late Paul Newman, and Martha Stewart (before she got run out of the place). I walked off the plane, covered head to toe with cold-deflecting clothes, but winters on the East Coast was like *nothing* I had *ever* experienced. The only way to describe it is, the cold went all the way through my hat, jacket, and sweater to my bones. But there Mike was, his green eyes twinkling and brilliant smile so bright, I was warm in an instant. The hour-long ride from JFK to Westport had my stomach in knots and needing to get to the nearest gas station bathroom.

If there was one word to describe what it was like meeting the In-Laws Karazin for the first time, it would be "awkward." Mike's mother, who had never associated with black people in her life, and his father, a judge, probably saw his share of trifling black folks and had his antenna up for any possible hoodrat-iness. Introductions went all around, and I was my friendliest, bubbliest self. Mikes father gave a terse greeting, little eye contact. We came right in time for dinner, but I can't remember what it was, only that it required seasoning. Dad Karazin barked, "Mom Karazin, fresh ground salt and pepper!" and she promptly passed them across the table to him. My eyes widened like saucers. I hadn't ever heard my father command my mother to do anything and I was honestly wondering what the hell kind of family this was.

Turns out Dad Karazin just likes fresh ground salt and pepper on his food. He probably was a bit uncomfortable, as was everyone else at the table, except for Mike, who says he doesn't remember being nervous. In fact, he can't remember a thing about that day, except for the meeting-me-at-the-airport part. I was grateful for bedtime, but the next day was worse. Someone—I can't remember who—made an offhand remark about black people and . . . I lost it. Not in front of them, but I excused myself to weep in Mike's older brother's childhood room. I cried, then I got it together. No one was mean, no one was rude, but they were clearly uncomfortable, and so was I. If it was going to be up to me to break the ice, I had the ice pick.

Reactions of the debut of your couple-hood to friends and family will range from the mild to the absolutely embarrassing and shocking. Jonathan Lee Gallup, fifty-seven, gave his future wife's eleven-year-old son (both black) a visual wallop. "She hadn't told him I was white. He walked around the corner, I took his hand to shake it, and he passed out on the sidewalk." I guess Jonathan's future stepson was shocked senseless.

Craig should probably have prepared Jayla a bit better, according to Dr. Tina Tessina, who specializes in romantic relationships. "Definitely prepare your family and your date in advance. Don't set this new person up to experience rejection, or a family disaster. If there's an issue, let your date know what the problems are, and if there are any real trigger issues to stay away from." ("Don't talk politics with Dad—he's a rabid right-winger; talk sports or hunting instead." "Mom will love you if you complement her cooking." "Do—or don't—offer to help Mom in the kitchen.")

Craig Murray's parents, mom from Jacksonville, Florida, and father from Ohio, knew his parents might have a problem with his new black girlfriend, Jayla. He tries to ease his mother into the idea gently.

"Well Mom, she's got a good tan, sort of exotic," he says.

"As long as she's not black," says his mother.

"You'll see."

And so she did, when Craig brought Jayla home in all her black glory, wearing Afrocentric attire and looking quite . . . black.

Craig should probably have prepared Jayla a bit better. "Their attitudes about black people were very similar to what mine had been in high school. It was less about 'blackness' and more about class." (Special thanks to Black Entertainment Television for making the world think black folks are a bunch of morons.)

Of course there was a bit of dismay at Craig's choice in women, since his last girlfriend had been blond, blue-eyed, and five-ten. But Jayla won them over with her energy and friendliness. One weird thing though: Even though Craig and Jayla had become engaged, his father still didn't allow her over for Christmas, which was "Murray clan only." It wasn't until the marriage was official did Craig's parents allow Jayla to fully participate in his family traditions. (Would it have been different if she had been white?)

Based on my experience and those of some experts I've consulted, there's an action list on how to handle this sort of race-tinged drama.

- **Gain some perspective.** The acceptance of interracial relationships is relatively new on the U.S. timeline. It wasn't until the late 1960s that black people and white people were allowed to marry. So chances are your rainbeau's parents witnessed the thicket of racial tensions and the transformation of certain institutions and programs. Some of them—myself included—never thought they would see an American president whose mother was a Midwestern white girl and whose father was Kenyan. That's a quantum leap from "Whites Only."
- **Be the antistereotype.** It's not fair that you have to be the official representative for all women of color, living or dead, but that's the way it is sometimes. If your boo's parents have a problem with your race, chances are they're just tapping into all the negative stereotypes they see about black women in the media. We're loud. We're fat. We roll our necks and emasculate our men. We have no class. We've heard it all before, and chances are his parents are shivering in their socks that you might be "that girl." Remember, the guy who's introducing you to his parents fell in like/love with you, so be that person—be you.
- **Relax.** This is better said than done, but it's an absolute must-do if you're going to keep your wits about you. But *stay away*

from liquid courage. If everyone is drinking, have one and babysit it through the whole dinner with a plain old water chaser. Thirty minutes of yoga before your date is equivalent to three beers without making you look like a drunken idiot.

- **Don't Go In with Your Boxing Gloves On.** I don't blame you at all if you're feeling a little defensive about proving yourself to your boyfriend's parents, especially if it's over race, a factor that you cannot change and cannot control. Tell your guy how you're feeling, but don't blame him for your uneasy feelings. This is a time for the two of you to present a united front. At the first meeting, be mindful of the defensive body language vibes you might be unconsciously sending. Those crossed arms and tight lip says more about you than the words that come out of your mouth. If someone says an, uh . . . off-color remark, now is not the time to challenge it. If they accidentally say "You people . . . " or "I knew a black person once!" the first meeting is not the right time to lecture your boyfriend's parents about their political incorrectness.

- **Come armed with lots of conversation.** Gather as much data about your rainbeau's parents before the actual meeting. Does his dad like to golf? Does his mother like to garden? Know about their work and hobbies and ask them about it. People *love* talking about themselves, and the more you keep them talking, the less time they will have to put *you* in the hot seat. Steer clear of potential hot buttons, like politics and religion. If the parents' questions to you starts to feel like a debriefing, answer the questions briefly, but then guide the conversation back to them. For example, if Mom or Dad ask, "So, Keisha, where are your folks from?" answer the question, then say something like, "My parents are from Kalamazoo, but I hear that your parents are from Europe. Have you been back to visit?"

- **Remember your table manners.** This goes without saying, but don't speak with your mouth full, keep your elbows off the table, try not to burp, but if you have to, do it into your napkin or cover your mouth with your hand, then say "Excuse me." Farting is completely out of the question.

What to Do if It All Goes to Shit

Chances are, everything will turn out fine and you'll leave your rainbeau's parents house with your head unchewed, your skin intact, and no shoe prints stuck on the back of your pants. But if things go terribly, terribly wrong, you and your boyfriend should have an exit strategy. Have a secret signal that you and your boo both know when it's time to exit stage left.

Run through a play-by-play of what happened. When you're calm enough to do it, have a talk with your guy about what he thinks went wrong, and how you felt about it. It might be hurtful, but it's important for you and him to communicate about the disaster. Why did it happen? How do you feel about it? How does he feel about it? Everything needs to be put out on the table, because what he does after the meeting could portend what things could be like in the future. If he is disquieted about the situation, don't be too defensive that he doesn't feel free to give you his take on things. For some men, family acceptance of a mate is paramount, so if his parents aren't accepting, there's a serious chance your relationship might be headed for a rocky road. You need to find out sooner than later where he stands. Try not to nag him about it, give him some space, and mostly watch his actions and behavior in the following days and weeks. If you feel he's cooling to you, it might be time to reevaluate your relationship, because that's a sure sign that the parents are winning.

Gary J. Hudecek, forty-seven, believes that the breakup of his fourteen-year marriage might be due in part to him not properly addressing the racial tension in his family. Gary's parents always knew he had a preference for dating black girls—and this was back in the 1980s—but never took his infatuations seriously until he announced that he was engaged . . . to a black woman with an eight-year-old boy from a previous marriage. There was mass hysteria in the Hudecek household, as everyone (except Gary) wrung their hands about what the extended family might think about their future daughter-in-law being black. It was 1989, he was twenty-five, and his parents refused to meet her until two days before the wedding. "The family pictures are funny—no one looked too happy," Gary recalls. He never really sat down with his parents and his wife about how shabbily they had treated his new bride, and she held on to that resentment for years. After the three additional children they had together, he talks of how he just wanted everyone to get along, play nice, and be the Cleavers. But Gary's wife never got an apology, and Gary never pushed for one. I can't stress it enough: Both partners must be unified and it must be clear as crystal that you two come as a package, or you won't come at all.

SUMMARY: DO'S AND DON'TS FOR MEETING THE PARENTS FROM DR. TINA TESSINA

DO: Wait until your relationship is getting serious before introducing your date to your family. If there's a family wedding or other event you want to bring your date to, clear it with your family in advance, if he or she hasn't been introduced yet.

DON'T: Just assume your date will know how to get along with your family.

DO: Explain how you relate to your parents. (e.g., "Dad and I get along better if we don't talk much.")

DON'T: Assume that your date's family relationship will resemble the one in your family.

DO: Give your date (if the relationship is serious) time to get to know your parents. If they're at a distance, include your new love in your letters or e-mails.

DON'T: Overreact to what your date or your family says or does. Everyone will be more calm if you are.

DO: Clue in your date about family customs—bringing a hostess gift when invited over, what they like to eat, what kind of humor they use, whether they play sports, cards, or board games together or discuss politics.

DON'T: Be too sensitive to what your date says about your family, or what your family says about the date, but do listen and think about it.

DO: Be as relaxed as possible, and let your date develop his or her own relationship with your family. Give them all time to get used to whatever is strange.

DON'T: Try to control what happens once you get there. You can be helpful, but don't try to force things to go the way you want.

DO: Talk about meeting family in advance—find out his expectations, share yours.

DON'T: Make too big a deal out of family—give each other a chance to figure it out.

DO: Think about what will work best for you and your date before you go.

DON'T: Expect your date to understand family quirks if they haven't been explained.

DO: Help your date fit in—suggest he help set the table, or talk sports with Dad.

DON'T: Ignore your date while you're with your family. You can talk to your sister, but make sure you check in with each other frequently, ask how your date is doing.

DO: Consider doing something that's time-limited and easier. If you go to dinner in a restaurant, everyone might be a bit better behaved.

DON'T: Hesitate to ask your partner how it was when it's over. A debriefing will help both of you.

CHAPTER SIXTEEN

Christelyn

Time to Decide:
Is It All Worth It?

Ah—the million-dollar question. With all we've been through in the previous chapters, I'll bet many of you will ask if all this swirly stuff is worth it. But even with all the coaching, cajoling, and personal stories, the answer ultimately depends on you, *chica*. But there is one thing I demand of you: Make it your choice. Not your mother's. Not your father's. Or Cousin Larry, Aunt Ethel, and/or your friends. It's okay to be afraid, as long as that fear doesn't cripple you.

Remember the classic Disney movie, *Dumbo*? Poor little thing thought he needed that feather to fly, but in the end—and with a little help from his friends—he realized all he needed was courage.

So you ask, "What if the people I love don't like my decision?"

I am reminded of a note I received from a young woman (let's call her Ramona) asking for my advice about what to do about her family's opposition to her interracial relationship. She was fretting at the level of negative opposition from the people closest to her. She was raised to be what she calls a "sister soldier," loosely defined as a black woman only interested in black issues, black people, external threats to black people, and uplifting her black brothers. "I was taught to live my life for the black community, only date black guys, and that white people were bad," she wrote. She was surrounded by female relatives involved in all manners of dysfunctional relationships—lying, cheating, deadbeat dads—but was taught by those women that being with a piece of a man is a noble sacrifice and dating outside would be a deep betrayal.

While away at college Ramona decided that she wanted more out of relationships that what she'd seen and heard. After attaining her degree and finding a career she enjoyed, she was reluctant to accept anything less than what her heart desired. "I spent two years away from home, lonely, sad, and in tears at night because I thought I'd never meet anyone who loved me and whom I loved in return.

Then she met a guy, a white guy who treated her like a queen and made her happy. Shocked and disgusted, her family now feels she has somehow abandoned them and the entire black community with her choice. "They say I've sold out, I'm 'whitewashed' and the people that I grew up with whom I love with all of my heart, including my parents, are treating me like some kind of leper." It seems that the family's processing is off, because they can't compute that Ramona can love a white man and still love her people.

Is loving someone a political statement, some outward display of allegiance and loyalty? Or is it just . . . love? You have to wonder about a family, friends, and community proscribes a woman from finding happiness with a man who lacks the proper melanin content. It's a cruel thought, isn't it? Almost makes you wonder about the intentions of the folks who are imposing such rules and sanctions, huh?

What I wish for every woman, man, girl, or boy who reads this book to do is adopt this credo, which so happens to be the hope of Dr. Martin Luther King Jr.: choose character above color—always and with every relationship you have. Color only goes skin deep. Character is as deep as the soul.

At this moment, I wonder how many readers are in Ramona's position, being forced to choose between family and racial loyalty over her own happiness.

You don't need Dumbo's feather to soar, ladies. Just the courage to spread your wings and fly.

Janice's Story

And She Lived Happily Ever After...

One of my favorite movies is *My Big Fat Greek Wedding*. The reception scene near the end of the film is particularly sweet. While toasting the marriage of his Greek daughter, Toula (played by Nia Vardalos) to Ian Miller, a non-Greek college professor (John Corbett), Gus Portokalos (Michael Constantine) raises his glass and with a serious brow, even though this had been a union he had vehemently protested, delivered this speech:

"I was thinking last night, the night before my daughter is going to marry *Ee-on Mee-ler*, that the root of the word *Mee-ler* is a Greek word. *Mee-ler* comes from the Greek word *Milo*, which means *apple*. As many of you know, our name Portokalos comes the Greek word *Portokilo*, which means *orange*. So here tonight we have apple and orange.

"We all different. But in the end, we all fruit."

Having watched the film again, just before writing this missive, I began thinking of the venerable mélange of fruits I have had over the years, with a handful of proverbial nuts. I'd dated white guys in college, but married a black man in 1992, which ended in divorce after eight years. Suddenly, nearing my midthirties, I found myself in the singles market again, and without much effort, attracting all sorts of shoppers in ways I had not imagined in my younger years. Not ready for another long-term deal, I suppose it was my ambivalence to a relationship that kept me in the constant company of men: black men, white men, my Persian computer instructor (who refused to identify himself as Iranian), and the Mexican flower vendor at my local farmers' market. As it happened, I asked him out after months of flirting amid the buckets of fresh sunflowers, stargazers, orchids, and peonies.

By the time I'd met the alluring man with the beautiful flowers it was 2010, just before spring, almost eighteen months since I'd ended a long on-and-off tryst with an actor who, as it was, happened to be black, and in between a string of a unsuccessful, albeit wildly memorable, hookups courtesy of match.com and eHarmony. The majority of my compatible online pairings were most often always with white men in their fifties or Asians in their thirties (figure that for a black woman in her early forties). And then there was that supremely bad blind date with a stoutly black musician who could never shut up; the first and last time I let friends play Cupid. As it happened, during the year I spent writing about swirling, so, too, did I swirl.

El Hombre de Flores

From the time I first began shopping at my local farmers' market, a few quick minutes browsing black calla lilies, a relationship quite literally blossomed over the following weeks. Our conversations would carry into the morning while shoppers headed away with their cellophane bundled blooms. By now, he knew I was a writer working on a film about jazz and shopping a book about dating out, and seemed to be as engaged by my stories as I was in him. He shared his secrets: longing to spend more time with his three-year old son, who was kept away by his fiery German ex-girlfriend; the close ties he had with his family in Ventura and back in Mexico where he was born. He often slipped me a few offerings from the bounty of sweet tomatoes, peppers, and cucumbers he had grown in his own organic garden because he knew I was partial to garden-grown grub. On those occasions when I had missed the market, he would pout and say he'd missed me. When I battled a mysterious monthlong bout of laryngitis, he mixed me a concoction of honey with orange, lemon, and lime. I had given him my phone number, at his request, so he could check up on me. But he didn't call. (He, of course, insisted he had; twice.)

I'd never been the aggressor in a relationship, believing the man should initiate traditional courting rituals. But here I was every Saturday morning, in the longest mating drought since my divorce, talking with this tall, tan, and muscular vision with wavy black hair that, when freed from the ponytail band he often wore, caressed his shoulders and back. And I knew I wasn't the only black woman in the neighborhood with an unrequited flower obsession.

A few months earlier, at the dawn of the New Year, I sat around a table with a group of black women, each of us designing our own dream boards that were to represent all the things we wanted to achieve in the coming year; a pastiche on cardboard to hang somewhere in the house as a reminder of the goals we had set for ourselves. The board I had created featured pictures of a surperbly fine man, jazz instruments, areas of travel, and the words "survivor," "storyteller," and "soul mate": my visual cues to be more open, to challenge my work, to love more, to live brave.

Had I become too much of a Black American Princess to consider starting something with a green-collar tradesman who had barely finished high school and was living with his sisters in a trailer park in the Ventura farmlands? Had I become intimidated by the idea that I was now one of *those* women who would prey on a younger man just for some temporary self-satisfaction? I had often considered my European and white girlfriends much more liberated when it came to this sort of thing. Just listening to my friend, Mo, talk of rendezvous with fellahs she'd entertained in Rome, in England, and wherever else in the world she's landed, even the most incompatible of men was more delectable than any of Elizabeth Gilbert's *Eat Pray Love* adventures. Would I be daring enough to do more than daydream about a fling with a pretty man who sold pretty flowers?

Apparently it would take some time. Beyond this tough, assertive independent veneer is a marshmallow. I'm not unlike most women: I prefer to be pursued. Two years of unintended celibacy was beginning to get on my nerves. I wasn't looking for marriage, or even what I'd consider a proper courtship. I didn't see the need to wait for fate or chance to dictate my next step: I just wanted out of the desert! Believing men typically want to be the hunters, I figured he would find my request for a date emasculating. But there was a slight chance he'd see it as endearing—maybe even sexy. Still, I prepared myself in case I would need to find another farmers' market for my Saturday morning shopping.

As August rolled around, just before my birthday, I asked him to dinner. He said yes; and he paid. And for the rest of the summer, I got my flowers delivered, but never again had to buy them.

Legal . . . Ease

Our shared passion for home cooking, great jazz, fast cars, and late-night walks along the South Bay beach proved no match for the ninety-minute drive from Ventura to L.A., the babymama drama with his ex, and the indecisiveness that oftentimes comes with a man just turning thirty. By late September—a season when lovely blooms begin to wither and fall from the trees—things were cooling off on my hot summer fling with *mi hombre de flores*. The Post-it with his number had gone into the trash. A few days later, at a business networking event in Santa Monica, I bumped into a lawyer.

I had read about these after-hours mixers in *Real Simple* and decided to go in hopes of drumming up new clients in need of a writer-for-hire, maybe land some corporate work outside the entertainment business, as assignments were getting increasingly fewer on my regular TV beat. Plenty of business cards were swapped that evening, but only a couple with intriguing prospects with whom I thought I could do some real business, including the attorney who had offered to buy me a drink. He said he had been waiting a half hour to talk to me.

He was, quite frankly, the answer to a prayer. A couple of days prior, I had received the contract for the book, with all the legalese the barristers of Simon & Schuster could muster. Christelyn, my beloved coauthor, still high from the acceptance, wasn't as concerned with all the graphs and clauses. Having known one too many author friends who had gotten the bum end of a publishing deal, I was fielding recommendations for someone who could review the contract on the cheap. And considering the aforementioned lull on freelance assignments at the time, pro bono was all I could afford. So far I had not found anyone who could go over those fifteen pages, and with only three days left to get my questions and revisions in, I was getting a little nervous. Okay, a lot nervous. I explained all of this to the attorney with alluring eyes and a handsome smile. "Send me the contract. I'll take a look at it," he said. Not picking up on the fact that he was now touching my arm, or that his eyes never once veered away from mine, my focus was only on how many billable hours these fifteen pages would cost me. "It's no problem. Just send it to me."

By the end of the week, I had notes and clarifications on the contract. And a dinner date. We met on a Thursday evening at The World Café in Santa Monica. I was, typically, ten minutes early; he was running fifteen minutes late. But I couldn't be too miffed when he eventually showed up, handsome in dark jeans and casual long-sleeve T-shirt that fit close enough for me to know he spends a considerable amount of time in a gym. Considering I was still high from having just secured another deal for my documentary the previous weekend in Monterey, I think I would have been okay if he had not shown up at all. After apologizing profusely for his tardiness, he hailed the waiter for wine recommendations. Not much of a social drinker—there is little I enjoy beyond a slushy margarita—I ordered lemonade with sparkling water. The attorney would educate me in "wine appreciation." I was intrigued, more by the premeditation of the offer than any need to become a lover of fine wine. The conversation was easy; there was much we had in common: politics, ambition, fitness, family. He was two years older, had never been married, and wasn't interested in it or having children but, after a series of online dates with women he considered shallow, he wanted something more serious in a relationship. He was the partner in his own small firm that was making some significant strides that year. And he appeared fascinated by my work and the trip to Monterey, and understanding more about jazz. I promised to teach him more about the music.

On our second date, a hike through the canyons in Malibu, he held my hand as we traversed steep cliffs and muddy terrain. Along the way, I stopped to snap a few digital stills of the scenery. At one stop, he asked someone to take a picture of us. Visually well suited, we are both of similar height (he is a tad taller)—lithe but athletic, with sharp features; my deep brown skin complementing his olive tones. Dark hair, dark eyes with a bold nose and thin lips, he could pass for Jewish, or possibly Iranian. His alpha-maleness suggests Latin or Italian. His last name: Anglo-Saxon. He takes great pleasure in being ambiguously ethnic: his mother is Italian, his father Mexican; his grandfather had changed the family name in order to pass for white when he came to America. Although he didn't want to be thought of as "just another white guy," the attorney knows no other language beyond English because his parents never spoke Italian or Spanish at home.

Date three: a quick bite, then a movie.

Date four: out to dinner then over to his place.

Date five: dinner at my place.

After the sixth date, I stopped counting. This was now the longest series of dates I'd had in a while (the flower guy only made it to five).

I delighted in telling friends about my new *thing*. It is how I have come to describe my courtship dalliances until I can call it love. A friend from high school cheered my "great catch" as I recounted over dinner the tales of my previous dates with the attorney, and she demanded to see the pictures from the hike. "Oh, Janice, you didn't tell me he was a white guy." Suddenly this good thing that I had was a huge disappointment to her. But I wasn't the one complaining about the dearth of available black men; of my fears about getting hurt again by yet another brotha who had done me wrong; of the extra pounds gained sitting at home alone on endless weekend nights with the dog, staring at the television; of a home with no children running around. She didn't understand why I would choose to date out. I didn't understand why she had chosen to marginalize her dating options.

We were the same on paper: having attended the same junior high school, the same high school; the same highfalutin, big-bucks, integrated private Southern California university; both professional women with entrepreneurial careers, and yet we could not have been more different in our views on race dating and mating. "I don't think I could _ever_ do that," she told me, before confessing she had dated another black woman's husband for several years.

Although I wasn't quite ready to label us _a couple_, the attorney and I were definitely doing all those things couples do. It was clear we wouldn't always agree on things and, admittedly, it took some getting used to the annoying pet names he'd chosen to call me: _doll, hon'_, and _pumpkin_ were his particular favorites. He liked to do more than hold hands in public, but I wasn't as comfortable with overt displays of affection around others. Despite his Latin bloodline, he still danced like a stereotypical, rhythmically challenged white college frat boy. (My ex-husband, the black guy, truth be told, wasn't much better.) I took pleasure instead in his attentiveness: the "just thinking about you, _doll_" e-mails in the middle of the day; the "I thought you'd like this" gifts, the dutifully opening of the passenger-side door of the car, the calls to make sure I made it home okay after a night at his place. He became my biggest cheerleader, always inquiring about, and finding interest in, my book and film projects. And when he didn't wig out after I whacked my midlength for a decidedly cropped pixie (he _loved_ it, in fact), I felt I had a keeper; and just in time for the holidays.

We made no formal plans for Christmas. Feverish with his

case load, and me busy interviewing subjects for the book and raising funds for my documentary, . . . *but can she play?*, for an early January film shoot in New Orleans, we had seen little of each other since Thanksgiving. I wasn't overly concerned that the random "thinking about yous" had waned. I had little time to do that for him. Now comfortable with one another, the natural relationship cycle began, it felt natural for me to now begin considering an appropriate *we've-been-dating-three-months-so-it's-not-that-serious-yet-for-me-to-buy-you-a-watch-but-I-wanted-to-show-you-that-I-care* gift to give him for the holiday. Following months of wine tutelage, I picked out a bottle of Italian chardonnay from Trader Joe's, purchased a divine dusty lavender designer dress shirt and tie at Nordstrom Rack, and painstakingly chose selected songs for a mixed CD compilation of jazz and coffeehouse tunes with a photograph of the Malibu mountains at sunset—thoughtfully packaged, and reasonably under seventy-five dollars.

Hitting the Skids

Six days into 2011, I had exchanged only a few e-mails with him over the holiday. We talked about getting together for dinner before Christmas Eve when he was planning to drive up to Central California to be with his family. Instead, he called me from the road a couple of days before. He decided to leave early. I invited him over for a New Year's Eve dinner. He had a long-standing ski trip to Mammoth scheduled with his buddies, though this was the first I had heard of it. Eventually the shirt went back to the Rack; the bottle of wine became a gift for my cousin (who loved it, by the way), and the CD, now boxed and ensconced in lily white wrapping with a shimmering silver bow, sat alone atop the piano waiting to be transferred into my own CD collection, or destroyed. Beyond differences in race or culture or faith, it is that other gender that boggles me; this man, who I had actually started thinking about introducing to friends, and perhaps even my mom and dad, was now giving off mixed signals. Was he just not that into me anymore? With less than eight hours before I was to board a flight for the Crescent City, I had little time for contemplation. I had a flight to catch and still needed to find $500 for the crew.

Against my better judgment, I decided to call him. When I got his voicemail, I almost hung up, but left a message to let him know I was leaving; that although I wanted to see him, I would catch up when I returned. He sent a text back almost immediately: He would be at my place by nine o'clock.

True to form, it was going on 9:30 when I heard the buzzer. I opened the door, and walked back toward the kitchen before he stepped into the foyer. I needed to separate my vitamins in their traveling case. I didn't care that he brought dinner for me, just in case I had gotten too busy to eat. I had not eaten. I just wanted to finish packing.

"You ready for your trip, *doll*?"

I wasn't ready for the trip, and even more unsure if I was happy he'd come. Before I knew it, I was vomiting up the bile of the day: my fears about the shoot, the online contracts that may or may not be legally binding, the ring I'd tried to sell and the money I still needed for the crew, and what happened over the holidays! It all came spilling out. He looked at me with a creased brow. I wanted to swallow my tongue, but it was too late. He could clearly see soft mushy marshmallow me.

He whipped out his wallet and emptied the contents of it into my hand. "There should be $200 there." He said he'd get more in the morning before I left. "Jesus, J, why didn't you tell me you were short."

"I didn't think we had that kind of relationship, considering . . ." As I was about to launch into a diatribe on holiday dreams deferred, I stopped myself, realizing that although I was still short on my budgetary goals, I now have enough to cover the camera crew. "I'll pay you back. I promise."

"It's not a loan. It's a gift," he said, explaining that he would have given me the money during my donation drive before Christmas, but had decided to wait and give me what I needed if I was running a little short. He then wrote down a number of a friend who lived in New Orleans in case I needed to connect with someone to help me navigate the city; he'd be expecting my call. Without hesitation, he then summoned me to retrieve the contracts so he could proof them. I returned with the papers, and the box with the CD, convincing myself that somehow it was worth more than what he'd just given me. He smiled as he stared at the cover: "This is really sweet, doll. Thanks."

That night we shared gyros and hummus in bed, while discussing where things were going between us. So far, it had been going great, we both agreed. Selfishly, I admitted, I wanted more of it more often. We talked about taking a couple of days in Santa Barbara, but in the weeks after my return from New Orleans, it became obvious that there would be no weekend rendezvous. There was no doubt we were compatible, but we just needed different things. He was now hopelessly devoted to his practice, having goofed off until his midthirties before getting serious about his career. I couldn't begrudge him that. Although my work was now in transition—for months I had grown more comfortable calling myself "filmmaker" and "author"—I had spent some twenty years as a journalist, twelve of those years hustling as a freelance entrepreneur. I had given so much of myself to the work. And in truth, I was ready, finally, to devote less of myself to it. I was ready to be somebody's girl. Instead, we decided to be friends, which for me meant we were done. There was no animosity, even though I was disappointed things hadn't gone better, but I had never been friends with an ex. Time spent in counseling over the years, both that of a spiritual and psychological nature, I've learned to move on rather easily.

Bringing It Back to Me

So where is my happily ever after? I'm living it, quite frankly. In the dozen years I've lived by myself, I have forged a great relationship with me. Cooking for one doesn't have to be a lonesome experience, but a culinary opportunity for me to experiment with all kinds of new recipes that suit, and challenge, my personal palate. Staying in my pajamas all day, lounging around in lingerie, or walking around naked, is my prerogative. I have no one to pick up after, no toilet seats to put down. Often I dance like nobody's watching: No one, as far as I know, actually is. There is a freedom every once in a while in letting go that connects me to the power, the beauty, and the whimsy that is me.

Close ties to friends and family keep my social calendar bursting, including the endless engagements of my young nieces. My home is a constant gathering place for large celebrations and intimate affairs: my hilltop no-drama zone that overlooks the city that I love, the mountains in the backdrop a constant reminder that there's something beyond. My work, and the travel it affords, opens me up to constant exploration; the engaging places and interesting people and furthering my connections to others that I might not otherwise have had the pleasure of knowing. I'm never wanting for the company of others. An ardent TV watcher from the womb, my pop culture icons that influenced me growing up—a pageant of self-sufficient black-and-white Barbies (with a dream town house and purple Corvette), Gidget (as played by a teenaged Sally Field), Marlo Thomas's *That Girl*, Mary Tyler Moore in *The Mary Tyler Moore Show*, and as I got older, *Murphy Brown*, and Oprah Winfrey—continue to resonate with me today: fiercely independent women who didn't shun the idea of having a mate, but did not allow their relationships with men to define them. I don't fear growing old alone, as many women I've known with children have done exactly that. It's the living with the "what ifs" that are scarier to me, always wondering what could have been instead of just doing it.

"When can I take you out?" It had been a little over a month since we split up when I got the call from the attorney, wanting to celebrate the trailer release of my film, which he had seen online. Twice I had avoided his e-mail invitations, but hearing his voice on the other end of the phone, so proud, it was difficult to say no. As I was changing into my fifth dress and my second pair of heels, I was wishing that he looked haggard; that the days since we had last seen each other had given him precious additional pounds. No such luck, of course. He looked delicious, and I was so nervous that, by the time we got to the restaurant, I could barely eat, I confessed. "Aw, J, what are you talking about? It's me!"

And it was: the same guy with the beautiful smile, the cheesy jokes, the attentive demeanor, easy conversation, and soft touch that endeared me to him from the very beginning. That guy who was content to let me be me, in pretty little dresses or my grungy little cotton gray shorts that he thought were so sexy; who would rather treat me to dinner than let me cook for him. That guy who would catch me when I fell. And I'd let him. (I didn't even let my ex-husband do that.) It was not long before the e-mails and calls started up again; we'd have late-night dinner deliveries, and on occasion he'd stay until morning.

We got together about a month before I left for Lake Arrowhead to finish the book. I was working late and he brought me dinner: a Cobb salad and chocolate chip ice cream. He stayed the night. I have not asked him where this was going, and I won't. The answer is not as important now. It's quite possible that I have gotten past romanticizing the possibilities of something more with him, in my head at least. The rest of me has yet to catch up. It's not that I don't miss him at times; I just don't dwell on it. Christelyn, bless her heart, is convinced, borrowing on an analogy from *Sex and the City,* that he's the Mr. Big to my Carrie. And it is not without precedent: men who vacillate over a relationship before realizing, finally, almost before it's too late, that they can't live without that woman. It was that way with her Michael, with whom she's been married ten years, raising a houseful of kids. My story will likely never end the way it did for Michael and Christelyn, or as it did for Ian and Toula. My relationship with the attorney could likely end up more like Jerry Seinfeld and Elaine Benes: lifelong pals who once upon a time had a *thing.* But with as many kinds of men in the world as there are fruit, I don't ever have to worry about a famine. I can have my pick of whomever I choose, enjoying each experience as it comes, and one more scrumptious than the next.

ACKNOWLEDGMENTS

Christelyn D. Karazin

I'm bound to forget something, so that's why my dependable coauthor will probably mention all those folks. Aside from the obvious—my agent, Regina Brooks; my friend and mentor, Janice Rhoshalle Littlejohn; and my ever-patient editor, Todd Hunter—I want to use this portion to thank a very specific group of women whom I've met online. These women have restored my faith in the existence of sisterhood. We band together for a common and simple wish: that black women will finally, and without guilt or regret, live life well. Cherilyn Smith (host of the blog *Black Women Deserve Better*) gave me my warm introduction to the online empowerment movement, where I found my voice and communed with some folks who were thinking what I was thinking and feeling what I was feeling and speaking up loudly and unapologetically.

Special thanks also to Lorraine Spencer, who put that little bug in my ear to make what first was a just a blog entry into an international movement that went viral, "No Wedding No Womb." I can't forget Lyn Twyman of the Courage Empowerment Network, a loving friend I met on Loving Day. To all the people who have shared your lives with me in hopes of helping and enlightening others, thank you. You're awesome. Special humongous thanks to Lori Thiel, who raked over some of my chapter with a fine-toothed comb and for giving my first platform in which I could showcase my voice way back when *[951] Magazine* was all the rage. Thanks Mom and Dad Karazin and Mom Russell for all the support and much needed funding during those lean months.

Finally, I want to thank every person who ever told me I couldn't do something, and all the people who helped me prove them wrong.

Let me not forget the man who is responsible for this journey, my life partner, Michael, "The Hubster" for those who follow my blog. He is responsible for much of the humor and wit you find in this book, because after fourteen years together, it was bound to rub off. I am in awe of what life we've forged together, and even through the tragedy and trauma, we found laughter, joy, and comfort. I love our little tribe. And despite the sleepless nights, mountains and landfills full of dirty diapers, and the baby running around holding a turd, I wouldn't change a single thing.

Janice Rhoshalle Littlejohn

A key element of this book is in the wide array of stories from the scores of couples and from black women who shared intimate details about their wonderful color-full, cross-cultural, and spiritually mixed romances. To my relatives, friends, colleagues, and neighbors who happily referred me to the people they knew, and to those who, for no compensation whatsoever, spent hours on the phone, online, or on Skype; who opened their homes and shared their lives and love stories with the no-holds-barred details that give this book an honest, forthright, and unique look into the joys and challenges of swirling, I am humbled and deeply appreciative of your contributions to this work.

But from the very beginning, this book has been a collective effort in which many have offered their expertise and skills. In our initial writing of the book proposal, my friend, and former *TV Guide* editor Rochell D. Thomas not only agreed to proofread and provide notes on an initial draft, but as Christelyn and I were racking our brains to come up with a catchy, succinct title, Rochell was the one who suggested we call it *Swirling*—especially since we had referenced it often throughout the proposal. I am forever grateful for her sage counsel, notes, and objective pair of eyes that helped to point out the obvious.

Regina Brooks, our agent, has been an unwavering champion of this project, helping Christelyn and I fine-tune the proposal, which lead to our signing with Atria Books in a matter of weeks. I am still amazed at how quickly she brokered the deal, and how she continued to shepherd the project throughout the process. As a first-time author, I valued and came to rely upon her expertise, and am so grateful to her for bringing us to Atria/Simon & Schuster—and to our editor, Todd Hunter. By far, a most easygoing, understanding, supportive, and for-real kind of guy, I cannot imagine having had a more exhaustively thorough, immensely patient, and wonderfully enjoyable editorial partner. Your feedback has been spot-on, and I am so grateful for the clear insight and direction you provided.

Many, many thanks to my forever friends in media and publishing: Earl Ofari Hutchinson, Brian Lowry, John Griffiths, Sherri McGee McCovey, Joshua Alston, Eric Deggans, and Mekeisha Madden Toby for their early support and public endorsement of the book; to my mentor—journalist, author, documentary producer, Jean Morris—for her wise counsel and encouragement. I still want to be you whenever I decide to grow up!

The process of bringing this work to fruition, despite having the counsel and collaboration of a writing partner, required countless days and nights—and wee-hours—spent alone, locked away in my office, or secluded in the mountains of Lake Arrowhead, the computer screen mocking my ability to construct a decent English sentence—much less an entire book. There were times that I simply could not make sense of anything that I wrote—and wondered if what was on the page made sense at all, and I am overwhelmed by the editorial support of my friend and go-to editing pal, writer Cherie Saunders, for all the times she poured through my chapters to make notes, offer words of encouragement, and get me back on track to begin again.

Josephine Thacker, who transcribed my many interviews, has not only been an administrative godsend, but has become a part of my special tribe of friends who are like family to me. Thank you for your tireless effort, weeding through the hours of tape-recorded conversations; for the conversations we shared together and for being such an enthusiastic cheerleader for "Team Littlejohn."

In a year that has had its share of personal and professional challenges, I am grateful to Jeannine Ginyard, Rochelle White, Angela Harris, Cheryl Robinson, Tracy and Sue Beidleman, Tracy Littlejohn, Catrina Smith, Michelle Love, Leon Brooks, Tiffany Stallworth, Christopher Fields, and James Michael Belk for their love, support, and many, many, many prayers and encouragement; for just listening to me fuss for a while about whatever I needed to get off my chest; and to "The Groovy Crew," my documentary team, who kept things going with the film when I had to switch gears and focus on this creative endeavor. It is because of each of you that I did not just spontaneously combust due to the stress and anxiety of bringing this project to fruition.

A special note of gratitude to graphic artist Adam Reid Janusz who enthusiastically took on the task of coming up with a design for the book cover; taking all of the wacky ideas inside my head of what I envisioned it could be and creating a beautifully concise, inspired work. I am in awe of your amazing talent, and thrilled to have had the opportunity to work with you on the book, and on the film; and am appreciative to your lovely wife, Saori Yunomura, for all the times she's allowed me to borrow you over the past year.

I am also exceedingly and abundantly appreciative to my coauthor and friend, Christelyn Karazin, for inviting me to collaborate with her on this project, and I am grateful to her for having confidence in my vision in and in my contribution to this effort.

My brother, Lonnie, and his family have also been greatly

supportive; and I appreciate his children—my nieces, Christina, Maya, and Angela, and nephew, Joshua—for being so forgiving of me having missed our annual beach outings during the summer I spent writing.

And albeit posthumous, I would be remiss if I did not acknowledge my great aunt, Hattie Mae Osment, to whom I first began writing stories, and my journalism instructor, Gwen Jones, who encouraged me to make a career of it—and what an exciting one it has been.

But more than anyone, I have to thank my parents, Jane and Londell Littlejohn, for . . . well, everything. After all these years, I still find myself depending on you both, and remain forever grateful for your being there, particularly in a year that has been most unusual—even for me. It is because of you I was able to make it through when, because of my focus on the book, my freelance work slowed, and times got really rough; making sure I had meals, when that plumbing snafu left me without a kitchen for the better part of five months; picking me up when I fell down (and, literally, could not get back up again after spraining my ankle from that unexpected tumble down the stairs); and always supporting my dreams, no matter how wacky they may seem—indeed, writing my first book and producing my first film all in the same year is pretty insane. Even for me. But then I've never been accused of being anything near normal. And I have you to thank for that, too.

RESOURCES

BLOGS

www.blackfemaleinterracialmarriage.com

dateawhiteguy.blogspot.com

lovingday.org

interracialdatingcoach.com

swirlingandmarriage.com

justlikemecouples.blogspot.com

lormarie.com

marriedgirlinaweirdworld.wordpress.com

whataboutourdaughters.com

yesweretogether.com

southafricangirlinsweden.wordpress.com

sojournerspassport.com

homespunwisdom.wordpress.com

aloftyexistence.wordpress.com

euphorialuv.wordpress.com

oneika-the-traveller.blogspot com

brooklyn-barcelona-belgrade.tumblr.com

lifebehindthewall.wordpress.com

survivingdating.com

acrushaday.blogspot.com

blackwomenlivingwell.wordpress.com

americanblackchickinlondon.blogspot.com

Isistheblogger.com

www.deedeerussell.com

bettychambers.com

socialitedreams.com

aloftyexistence.wordpress.com

blackfemininity.com

www.cocoafly. com

smelodydiva.wordpress.com

politicallyunapologetic.com

BOOKS

Is Marriage for White People?: How the African American Marriage Decline Affects Everyone, Ralph Richard Banks

Don't Bring Home a White Boy: And Other Notions that Keep Black Women From Dating Out, Karen Langhorne Folan

Kissing Outside the Lines, Diane Farr

Black Woman Refined, Sophia Angeli Nelson

Dating the Ethnic Man: Strategies for Success, Faizal Sahukhan, PhD